Finally Truffaut

Cher Don, pourquoi ne demandez-vous pas à S & W de vous laisser "actualiser" votre livre sur mon travail? Moi aussi je vous souhaite une bonne et heureuse année 79,

amitiés

françois truffaut

François Truffaut to Don Allen

# Finally Truffaut

## Don Allen

Secker & Warburg
London

First published in England under the title *François Truffaut*
by Secker & Warburg in 1974
This revised edition first published in England 1985 by
Martin Secker & Warburg Limited
54 Poland Street, London W1V 3DF

Copyright © Don Allen 1974, 1985

British Library Cataloguing in Publication Data

Allen, Don
   [François Truffaut] Finally Truffaut.
   1. Truffaut, François—Criticism and
   interpretation
   I. [François Truffaut]  II. Title    ·
   791.43′0233′0924    PN1998.A3T7/

   ISBN 0–436–01180–8

Filmset in Photon Times 11 pt. by
Richard Clay (The Chaucer Press) Ltd, Bungay, Suffolk
and printed in Great Britain by
Fletcher & Son, Ltd, Norwich

# Contents

# Introduction

'Truffaut's friendship, once given, was for life' – Suzanne Schiffman.

I had the privilege of knowing François Truffaut over a period of fifteen years, from the time of our first meeting in 1969 to his untimely death in 1984. Our relationship was unique 'in its own way', just as every woman is unique, as Fabienne Tabard says in *Baisers Volés*, 'each in her own way'. Truffaut's gift for friendship made every one of his friends feel special.

Over the years I spent many hours in his company, interviewing him in his apartment, his car, his office at Les Films du Carrosse and on stage at the National Film Theatre in London. We ate and talked together – though the eating for Truffaut was never more than a necessary evil – in the restaurants of large hotels, in small bistros and in his own home. I was present at the shooting, viewing of rushes, post-synchronization and premières of many of his films. Chabrol's tribute to Truffaut in relation to his friends in the French New Wave, 'We all owe him a little for being able to start off as we did', can be echoed by many actors and actresses, film-makers and writers throughout the world, and certainly by myself. I too received from him a mass of correspondence and also books, scripts and articles written by or about Truffaut or those whose work he admired. He read my articles and encouraged me to write my first book on him in 1974. Later in 1979 while writing the preface for my *Book of the Cinema*, one of several prefaces he wrote for projects he approved, he asked the question on the frontispiece to this book: 'Why don't you ask Secker and Warburg to update your book on my work?' The answer, rather belatedly, is this present work.

Truffaut's concept of friendship did not preempt fierce criticism of those whom he loved. André Bazin, Jean-Pierre Léaud, Jeanne Moreau and many others bear witness to the demanding nature of his friendship. A condition of entry into Truffaut's universe was that you were prepared to accept his lucid yet passionate judgments in the spirit of 'Whom the Lord loveth, He chasteneth'. This present book is written in the same spirit. A small number of films seem to me to be quite flawed, others marginally so, as Truffaut, always his own worst critic, was the first to admit. On the other hand some of his best films stand comparison with the best of world cinema and are rightly seen as masterpieces. Above all, viewing his work as a whole, as this book seeks to do, there can be little doubt as to the validity of Truffaut's claim to a place in the pantheon of the world's best-loved directors.

This book assumes that readers will have seen many of Truffaut's films but not necessarily all of them, so some sort of plot outline is contained within each chapter. The films are treated in chronological order – with the exception of the five films in the Antoine Doinel cycle – and one chapter is allocated per film in order to help the reader who wishes to study one film in isolation. The danger of this approach is of course to focus attention on an individual film rather than on the 'oeuvre' as a whole, with consequent loss of continuity and thematic unity. This is offset by drawing attention to the way themes recur throughout the films – fundamental to any 'auteurist' approach – and by emphasizing the echoes and resonances – of a personal, literary and cinematic nature – which permeate Truffaut's whole work. Although the Antoine Doinel films are grouped together, partly because of the clear autobiographical links – which are discussed in Chapter Four by means of an examination of some of the evidence available on Truffaut's jealously guarded private life – we need also to be aware of the extremely strong autobiographical thread running throughout his work. In an interview in *Le Monde* in 1971 Truffaut even states that he is more intimate and sincere in the films outside the Antoine Doinel cycle: 'I have a great tendency to talk about myself, and a very great revulsion against doing so directly.'

Truffaut's films then are always about himself – in varying degrees and more obviously in some films than others. They are also always about love, in some form or other. The typical Truffaut

François Truffaut and Don Allen at the British première of 'Le Dernier Métro'

hero contains many of his creator's personal characteristics and will be involved in some sort of love relationship. His early short film *Les Mistons* announces these themes and they are developed at length in the remainder of his work. The themes may be variously subdivided. For example, the importance and difficulty of friendship, especially male friendship; the role of women – are they magic? are they unique? are they dream goddesses, mother figures or whores? – the fascination with language and especially the written word; the conflict between the provisional and the definitive; the obsession with obsession; the complete intoxication with cinema and the tendency to take refuge in it as being 'more harmonious than life'; the increasing preoccupation with absolutes.

The view of life that emerges from Truffaut's films is one of muted pessimism – or muted optimism for those who prefer to consider the pot half-full. Life is shown as being worth living but none of the pain or isolation is minimized. Sometimes Truffaut seems naïve in his ability to shut out from his universe, as for example in *L'Enfant Sauvage*, any consideration of the negative aspects that are the corollary of a passion. Thus he appears to approve of the partially successful attempt to civilize the wild child and to endorse the desirability of the experiment, as if oblivious to the possibility of questioning the aims and the methods of an experiment based on nineteenth-century pedagogical notions as to the increased happiness of a forcibly indoctrinated 'savage'. Truffaut's passion for education, as an unquestionable good, blinds him to all other arguments.

Truffaut is aware of the need to lighten the tone before he reaches the end of some films and he strives never to finish on a downward note. Sometimes he merely mixes the tones – as in the interpolation of comic banter into the melodramatic love story involving two deaths in *Tirez sur le Pianiste*. There is frequently a tone of overriding melancholy, but lightened by humour and bitter-sweet episodes illustrating the idiosyncracies of human behaviour.

Mitigated pessimism about the human condition is a factor in most of Truffaut's films. 'L'amour fou', absolute and uncondi-tional, is doomed to failure – Fabienne Tabard and 'the man in the mac' in *Baisers Volés*; Louis in *La Sirène du Mississippi* (apart from the artificial and unconvincing ending); Adèle in *Adèle H.*; Julien in *La Chambre Verte* and so on. The compromises which are possible within the frustrations and limitations of marriage are not passionately endorsed by Truffaut – notably in *La Peau Douce, Fahrenheit 451, Domicile Conjugal, L'Amour en Fuite* and *La Femme d'à Côté*. Adultery or 'open triangles' fail ignominiously or magnificently – *La Peau Douce, Jules et Jim, Domicile Conjugal, Les Deux Anglaises et le Continent* – though the problem is left unresolved in *Le Dernier Métro*. The safety-in-numbers solution hinted at in the literary commune at the end of *Fahrenheit 451* and lived with obsessive determination by Bertrand in *L'Homme qui Aimait les Femmes* isn't shown as exactly life-enhancing and ful-filling. In over half the films death plays a significant part. In many a character is left alone at the end. Truffaut's early conclusion: 'The couple solution does not work and there are no other solu-tions' applies as much to the later films as the early works.

Truffaut's own solution to the imperfections of life was to take refuge – from his childhood to the time of his death – in the cinema.

Within this world he was safe and he took care never to stray far outside it into a world he could not control. He made films, saw films, talked about films, planned films and lived films to the virtual exclusion of everything else. His relationships with women were usually with actresses, who were thus all part of this closed cinematic universe. Political and social themes were of no interest. Politicians were seen as a necessary evil, like housekeepers: needed to empty the ashtrays and keep things in order, but whose value should not be exaggerated. Social change was best brought about as slowly as possible and all revolutions were subject to equally dramatic reversal, examples of which he could readily quote.

So the man whose self-confessed religion was Charlie Chaplin, devoted himself to the making of films about the only subject that really interested him and on which he was an undoubted master – that is the relationships between human beings. In his love of humanity he is sometimes in danger of being over-compassionate, in keeping with his favourite maxim from Renoir about people always having their reasons. 'People are fantastic,' asserts Fabienne Tabard and Truffaut seems to concur. Truffaut depicts the minute fluctuations of emotion, the ebb and flow of confidence, timidity, affection, passion. His work reaches audiences worldwide because of its concentration on the universal human experience. The judgment of posterity will surely be that he is one of the most important names in the history of the cinema.

# 1: Grave-digger to Film-maker

This above all to thine own self be true.
And it must follow as the night the day,
Thou canst not then be false to any man.
                                        *Hamlet*

Some misconceptions about the work of Truffaut the film-maker arise directly from the career of Truffaut the critic. And Truffaut's formative years as a critic are a necessary point of departure in any assessment of his films. In 1952, thanks especially to the help of his mentor and surrogate father André Bazin, Truffaut was appointed film critic for the French cultural magazine *Arts*, and also began to write regularly for *Cahiers du Cinéma*. Thus began the flow of articles, reviews and interviews which deluged the French intellectual public in the late Fifties and early Sixties, diminishing, as Truffaut's own film output increased, to the occasional article in *Cahiers* by the late Sixties.

In the mid-Fifties, together with his *Cahiers* colleagues Doniol-Valcroze, Rohmer, Rivette, Godard and Chabrol, Truffaut saw much to destroy. Passionately, flamboyantly, he set about destroying it. He became known as 'the grave-digger of the French cinema', hated by those he attacked, revered and esteemed by those who shared his views. In 1958 Doniol-Valcroze said of him: 'In a few years François Truffaut has become the most famous of the young film critics. What many muttered under their breaths he dared to say out loud ... He has firmly kicked the conformist backside of the French cinema.'

The main target for Truffaut's toe was the hidebound French cinema of the Forties and early Fifties. An unequivocal one-line notice, 'In not seeing *Chéri-Bibi* you will doubtless spend an excellent evening,' a provocative 'There is nothing more to say of *Futures Vedettes* except that the French cinema will produce many more films of this "non-quality" until the public learns to choose and

Father figures: André Bazin (with Alexandre Astruc), Jean Renoir and Alfred Hitchcock

eventually to smash the seats,' sufficed to dismiss the dross. The gold was to be found among the seventeen directors Truffaut had placed in the 'ambitious' section of his classification of ninety-nine French directors, which he drew up in 1955. The other three sections consisted of the 'semi-ambitious', the 'honourably commercial' and the 'deliberately commercial'. This rigid schematization did not, however, ensure automatic praise even for the seventeen directors in Truffaut's personal pantheon.

Truffaut's invective frequently involved quite vicious personal attack. In a review of *Chiens perdus sans collier* (1955), he wrote: 'The whole is written to order for the Gaumont-Palace by two disillusioned and cynical scriptwriters – Jean Aurenche and Pierre Bost, who have written "touching" dialogue – and is set to images by a man insufficiently intelligent to be cynical, too crafty to be sincere, too pretentious and solemn to be simple, Jean Delannoy.' Claude Autant-Lara was similarly pilloried, not merely for his 'truculence, vulgarity, exaggeration' and his resemblance to a butcher who persists in doing fine embroidery, but also, and particularly, because he is only a diligent *metteur en scène* of scripts written by others; he is not a film author but an 'illustrator of texts'. 'Autant pour Lara', one of Truffaut's more forgettable puns, was the punchline to this particular polemic.

The word 'revolutionary' might be applied to Truffaut in two senses only. First because he was committed to the violent destruction by spectacular critical attacks of what he judged bad; secondly, and more literally, because 'revolution' for him has implied turning the wheel back to his cinematic golden age, the Thirties. The cinema which Truffaut advocates is firmly based on the best characteristics of this period, and in particular on the total authorship and consequent directorial freedom of such lyrical film creators as Jean Renoir and Jean Vigo. Truffaut alternates vigorous attacks on partial creators and production line commercialists with equally militant defence of independent film-makers. It was largely as a result of the perceptive exegeses and initial pioneering publicity of Truffaut and his *Cahiers* colleagues that American directors such as Hawks, Walsh and Fuller, who had formerly been identified in the public mind, if at all, as part of the Hollywood machine, were raised to *auteur* status. In addition, an enthusiasm was generated for the American B-picture, which was to exercise a strong influence on

13

The American connection: gangster film pastiche in *Tirez sur le Pianiste*

Truffaut and Godard in particular and to provide them with the framework and background for several of their films. In Truffaut's case, *Tirez sur le Pianiste*, *La Mariée était en noir*, *La Sirène du Mississippi* and *Vivement Dimanche* are inconceivable without his exposure to the American cinema in the late Forties and the Fifties. Together with *Fahrenheit 451*, these films constitute what might be called the 'American' strand in Truffaut's work. They reflect predominantly the influence of Hollywood and in particular of Hitchcock, though the Hitchcockian influence is discernible in other films. The rest of Truffaut's work, particularly the Antoine Doinel films, might be regarded as part of the French lyrical tradition; and the specific influence here is Renoir.

Hitchcock is the subject of Truffaut's full-length interview book,* published in 1967 after some fifty hours of interviews

* *Hitchcock*, Simon and Schuster, New York, 1967; Secker and Warburg, London, 1968 revised 1978 (Paladin) and reissued 1985.

recorded in 1962, when Truffaut was already celebrated as a director. The book is scarcely the definitive study of Hitchcock; Truffaut revealed greater critical insight elsewhere, notably into Hitchcock's macabre humour as revealed for example in *Rear Window*. The essential Hitchcock is never probed, remaining elusive behind the showman, raconteur, auto-publicist façade. Indeed, the main interest of the work lies in what it reveals of Truffaut's own preoccupations as a film-maker. Hitchcock, for Truffaut, emerges as the technical oracle to be consulted, the box of tricks to be ransacked. It is verification of detail, establishment of how shots and effects were achieved, which fascinates Truffaut. He had already assimilated many of the views Hitchcock expresses here, for example the fear of generating boredom, the need to entertain and therefore consciously to manipulate audience reaction. When the occasional disagreement does emerge, Truffaut is too reticent and Hitchcock too experienced at interviews for the point to be forced home. Hitchcock's outright commercialism is never challenged, nor his dismissal of the actor's role ('The chief requisite for an actor is the ability to do nothing well'). It is characteristic of a book which is more admiration than criticism that when on the penultimate page Hitchcock admits to a major weakness in his work, the 'thin characterizations within the suspense stories', Truffaut never follows it up, indeed does not even think it worthy of comment.

The evolution of the New Wave phenomenon coincided of course with the development of the *auteur* theory, and Truffaut's role in the promotion of both was decisive. The cumulative flow of his years of criticism led naturally to his 1958 manifesto, which became almost a working document for the New Wave. Studios were too expensive, so the film of tomorrow was to be shot entirely on location, in the streets, on the beaches, with natural décor and lighting; dialogue would not be the stilted and stylized product of a professional scriptwriter, but the conversation the film-maker might have had with his wife the night before, or even conversation improvised by the actors; films would be made quickly and cheaply; the film-creating process was to be demythologized so that anyone could pick up a camera and shoot a film as he might pick up a pen and write a novel. In this way a climate of opinion was established in which the New Wave could flourish. Truffaut's contribution is reflected in

Chabrol's testimony: 'Look what Truffaut has done. Things got stirred up. We all owe him a little for being able to start off as we did.'

Truffaut remained remarkably consistent, even static, in his cinematic judgments over the years, continuing to defend the kind of cinema he was defending in 1955. But he did know the critic's occasional blush of shame. 'Often people quote at me some of the things I wrote and that embarrasses me greatly,' he said in connection with his oversimplification of the technical problems of film-making, which led to the excess of freewheeling camerawork, shots of beaches and sunlight, and slack editing soon to become the trademarks and the clichés of the New Wave. One inconsistency does emerge in Truffaut's attitude to the Cannes film festival. In his early days as a critic Truffaut scathingly dismissed the mediocrity of Cannes; banner headlines ('Cannes — a failure dominated by compromise, scheming and blunders') heralded a fierce denunciation of the festival which brought protests even from Henri Langlois of the French Cinémathèque and resulted in Truffaut being overlooked by the organizers of the 1957 festival; which did not stop him attending, signing his articles 'François Truffaut, the only critic not invited to the festival'. Two years later things had changed. Truffaut's first feature, *Les Quatre Cents Coups*, was shown at Cannes as the official French entry, and Truffaut accepted the Grand Prix for the film. In 1962 he was a member of the festival jury.

No one rises in a few years from anonymity to celebrity with innocence intact. But it would be misleading to accept the caricature of Truffaut as a young *arriviste* with an eye to the main chance, as some critics have done, simply because his vituperative style as a critic led to rapid public recognition and ultimately, helped by his marriage to Madeleine Morgenstern, daughter of one of France's richest and most powerful distributors, to his progress from critic to film-maker. One such critic, Henri Jeanson of *L'Aurore*, writing in 1969, accused Truffaut of merely mouthing such words as 'purity, honesty, frankness, innocence' and even claimed that '*tendresse*', the word most generally associated with Truffaut, is 'nothing but a publicity stunt'.

Truffaut certainly never disguised the fact that his intention, his dream, was to make films, and that his film reviews were increasingly an account of what he would have done with the material rather than

16

The New Wave at Cannes, 1959 (Truffaut on left of front row)

film criticism proper: 'I loved the cinema passionately enough not to remain a spectator.' As Doniol-Valcroze recalled in 1958: 'If he so often attacked, scorned, slandered what he did not like, it was because he wanted to do what he did like.'

A common reaction to Truffaut's films is a sense of anticlimax, prompted by the discrepancy between what Jean Curtelin has called his 'blustering declarations and his slender final baggage'. The most serious charges of all are made by those who either misunderstand or dismiss as irrelevant Truffaut's contribution to cinema. For such critics it is not enough for him to say that he did not want to change cinema but only to continue to make better examples of the kinds of film he enjoyed seeing in his youth. His indiscriminate attacks as a critic on the 'bourgeois' and 'petit bourgeois' film-makers – words which he never defined – were not surprisingly taken for authentic revolutionary language. People looked to him for committed, political films – and found him wanting. By this criterion, even if he is not the Jean Delannoy of the New Wave, he is clearly, again in the

17

words of Curtelin, 'the *enfant terrible* confined within the bounds of bourgeois respectability'. The apparent revolutionary is only a rebel after all.

Fortunately, Truffaut's claim to originality is not affected by the absence in his films of revolutionary innovation on either a technical or a political level. He must be judged by other criteria.

# 2: Les Mistons

A film director's total work is a diary kept over a lifetime.
François Truffaut

Jean Renoir said that throughout his career a director makes only one film. The others are merely remakes, reworkings of the themes contained in that first film. Truffaut subscribed to this idea, and did so consistently from his period as a critic up to his death. And in his first film, *Les Mistons*, one finds the thematic and stylistic embryo of his later work. Truffaut himself, whose capacity for self-criticism verges on the masochistic, thought that the critics who praised *Les Mistons* were very indulgent, and sympathetic to his intentions rather than his achievement.

Certainly the main interest of this first film lies in its germinal nature and in the light it throws on Truffaut's later work, rather than in its inherent qualities as cinema. The film was financed largely by Truffaut's wife, and shot on location at Nîmes in 1957 with the help of a few friends (notably Claude de Givray) and with five local boys as the *mistons*. Truffaut took the idea from a short story in *Les Virginales* by Maurice Pons. Despite this reliance on an existing source, and the co-operation of its author, Truffaut's adaptation emerges as the work of one man and carries his total directorial imprint.*

The film deals with the awakening sexuality of a gang of twelve-

---

*This, of course, is the essence of the *politique des auteurs* theory, as Peter Wollen has shown in *Signs and Meaning in the Cinema* (1969, Secker and Warburg, London): 'The director does not subordinate himself to another author; his source is only a pretext, which provides catalysts, scenes which fuse with his own preoccupations to produce a radically new work.'

year-old boys during a long summer in Nîmes, as they become increasingly fascinated by Bernadette, the sister of one of them, and her love affair with Gérard, 'un drôle de type' who teaches physical education at the local lycée. The boys seek to compensate for the fact that they are too young to love Bernadette by waging war on the couple, spying on them and harassing them. Gérard is killed in a climbing accident, and the film closes on a melancholy note.

The original running time of twenty-six minutes was subsequently cut by Truffaut to seventeen minutes. In this way he hoped to prune some superfluous dialogue and also to moderate the film's main weakness, which lies in the over-explicit, rather wooden commentary. This commentary reflects both Truffaut's literary origins as a film critic 'who would have written novels were it not for the cinema' and also his over-anxious desire for complete clarity in his films. But here pruning was an inadequate remedy. Tinkering about with the overstrained heart of the film is no help in a situation which calls for a transplant. The verbosity could only have been replaced by visual clarity. Hitchcock's precept, 'Whatever is said, instead of being shown, is lost upon the viewer', is here neglected by one of its firmest advocates. The ineptitude of the American paraphrased version of the commentary is a further hazard for English audiences.

*Les Mistons* is Truffaut's gaze through a nostalgic filter at his own and Everyman's adolescence. His personal tone permeates Maurice Pons' story, rather as Alain Resnais' individual ethos powerfully transcends each of his diverse novelist scriptwriters. In subject and mood the film closely anticipates the more directly autobiographical *Les Quatre Cents Coups*, and thus serves as a kind of preface to the Antoine Doinel cycle. It has all the awkwardness and grinding sincerity of an experimental first exercise, yet it reveals almost everything about its author: his timid, voyeuristic adoration of 'Woman'; his fondness for bitter-sweet nostalgia, in which surface humour alleviates sadness and tenderness tinges passion; a charm and lightness of touch which eschews analysis and probing; a cinematic culture underlying almost every shot and made explicit in a direct homage or an in-joke; an instinctive anticipation of audience reaction and desire to entertain, while remaining 'sincere'.

The prototype for the later diffident, vulnerable, woman-dominated Truffaut hero is to be found in the composite portrait of the *mistons*. Men are seen from the imagined viewpoint of the woman, as little boys playing games, driven on by half-understood passions, innocent victims shaped by the whim of woman, the unattainable siren and implacable love goddess. This gang of adolescents sees Bernadette as the exciting forbidden fruit, the enigmatic flower of their shameful dreams. It is not yet 'Vénus toute entière à sa proie attachée', but the symptoms are there. Incipient passion, frightening and unknown, is channelled into hatred; group solidarity emboldens faint hearts. The Don Juan syndrome asserts itself, as these former victims of the will of woman become the aggressors and begin to think in the terminology of the military campaign. The female, Bernadette, becomes the enemy; war is declared, and Truffaut unsubtly points the moral with close-ups of a female praying mantis devouring a male in copulation.

The news of Gérard's death — movingly conveyed by three superimposed dissolves of newspaper headlines (anticipating *La Sirène du Mississippi*) and a long-shot of people in mourning emerging from church (anticipating *La Mariée était en noir*) — imposes a solemnity on the end of the film. The fundamental dichotomy between lust and 'true love' is highlighted by shots of prostitutes, full-breasted women and pouting lips, intercut on three occasions with a slow-motion, almost frame by frame close-up of Gérard and Bernadette kissing in profile, an image of tenderness rendered more poignant by the recent news of his death. Then Truffaut, sensing that we are verging on tragedy, as usual lightens the mood — while retaining the thematic thread — with a shot of a voluptuous Brigitte Bardot on a poster for Vadim's *Et Dieu créa la Femme*, and in front of it a *miston* shaking his fist because the film is forbidden to those under sixteen. Other comic interludes, such as the jerkily edited, slow-motion business with the gardener and the hosepipe (a homage to Lumière) and the gag with the man who when asked for a light says aggressively that he never gives one, are simply comic relief inserts, related to nothing except Truffaut's repertoire of cinematic memories and his often expressed show business desire 'never to have two elephant acts running'. The epitome of this particular Truffaut trick is the celebrated flash shot of the gangster's mother dropping dead in *Tirez sur le Pianiste*.

The whole film can be seen as an extended homage to Jean Vigo. Not merely in its specific references to *Zéro de Conduite* in the dialogue and the camerawork (one shot of the *mistons* silhouetted against the town wall recalls Vigo's shot of the pupils in revolt on the school roof), but in its treatment of love, its gentle humour and its lyrical tone. More generally, the proliferation of cinematic allusions and cross-references with which all Truffaut's films are studded is one of the hallmarks of the New Wave. Sometimes the effect is to reinforce the theme; for example, during the obligatory cinema sequence here, when on the screen the woman in Jacques Rivette's *Le Coup du Berger* (Truffaut often plugs his friends' films) is on the point of succumbing to Jean-Claude Brialy and Truffaut cuts to Gérard and Bernadette embracing in the audience. Elsewhere the allusion takes the form of a gratuitous in-joke, for example when the *mistons* steal a poster of Jean Delannoy's *Chiens perdus sans Collier*: Truffaut, despite having previously slated the film, is still unable to let sleeping dogs lie. Other quirkily irrelevant sequences, like the bitter-sweet anecdote of Bernadette's uncle and the boil which blighted his love prospects, are included because Truffaut cannot resist them. They are on a par with the love by correspondence story in *Jules et Jim* – isolated, whimsical comments on the foibles of circumstance. Scenes such as the violent cuffing of one of the *mistons* by Gérard anticipate the striking of children in *Les Quatre Cents Coups* and *L'Enfant Sauvage* and are clearly a personal reminiscence for Truffaut, for whom adolescence was 'a bad moment to get through'.


During the winter following the shooting of *Les Mistons*, Truffaut was involved in a project which was eventually completed by Godard. The genesis of *Une Histoire d'Eau*, as this short film came to be called, could scarcely have been more casual. Always, he says, fascinated by floods, Truffaut took the opportunity of floods on the outskirts of Paris to ask Pierre Braunberger, the producer, for some spare film stock so that he could film a *fait divers* with two actors, Jean-Claude Brialy and Caroline Dim. When he got to the floods he was a little reluctant to make the film at all in view of the seriousness of the situation for the flood victims. But he shot some footage, and then did nothing more with it. Godard later took over the film, edited it, and supplied a laconic commentary. This droll, if not moral, tale is in fact co-signed by Godard and Truffaut, but Truffaut's collaboration ended with the shooting.

Influences: (*above*) Hitchcock (*La Mariée était en noir*); (*below*) Renoir (*Jules et Jim*)

23

The film chronicles the experiences of a couple cut off by the floods from the road to Paris. They talk and eventually make it (he: 'together'; she: 'to Paris'; in both senses in fact), and that is the kind of pun with which the film abounds. With its deadpan, offbeat humour, tortuous puns, intellectual asides, atmosphere of sexual amorality and mood of anarchy, the film anticipates *A Bout de Souffle*. Certainly Truffaut's sweeping camerawork, particularly the aerial shots, contributes to the fairytale atmosphere (to be recaptured in *Jules et Jim*), and, in an aside to the audience, Godard acknowledges the debt: 'Normally I don't give a damn about the image; it is the text which is important. But this time I am wrong, because here everything is beautiful.' All the same, *Une Histoire d'Eau* has Godard stamped all over it, and it cannot really be considered a Truffaut film.

# 3: The continuing story of Antoine Doinel

Truffaut's own statement that 'one is always autobiographical but one is so to a greater or lesser extent' can be applied more readily to himself than to most other directors. With Truffaut the autobiographical element in his work is of major importance. He is always present in his films, even though his major personal appearances number only three, – in *L'Enfant Sauvage*, *La Nuit Américaine* and *La Chambre Verte*. Sometimes he expresses and thus reveals himself through one of the minor characters; more often he does so through the hero. This is particularly the case in the Antoine Doinel cycle, with Jean-Pierre Léaud.

When interviewed, Truffaut was very reticent about the details of his private life; but from the facts that can be gleaned the parallels between his own life and that of his fictional creation overwhelmingly support the view that, at least on an autobiographical level, Antoine Doinel *is* initially François Truffaut. Like Antoine, Truffaut was an only child, had a wet-nurse and was brought up by his grandmother until the age of eight, when his parents took over, though they were too occupied with their own problems to bother much with their child. Truffaut's father's fascination with camping is echoed, in *Les Quatre Cents Coups*, the first of the Doinel films, by Monsieur Doinel's obsession with car rallies. Again, Truffaut was expelled from a succession of schools, from which he had frequently played truant and gone on clandestine trips to the cinema with his friend Robert Lachenay; Antoine does likewise with his friend René Bigey. Antoine and Truffaut both discover Balzac at an early age and are fired with an enthusiasm which continues into their adult lives.

*Les Quatre Cents Coups*: clandestine cinema-going (Jean-Pierre Léaud, Patrick Auffay)

Truffaut, like Antoine, committed petty crimes, ran away from school and home, lived for a time with his friend's family, was turned over to the authorities by his father, and was sent to the Reform School for Juvenile Delinquents at Villejuif.

Antoine runs away. We learn from the outline for the script of *Antoine et Colette*, the second chapter in the Doinel story, that he is brought back and finally released, thanks to the efforts of the sympathetic woman psychiatrist in *Les Quatre Cents Coups*. At sixteen, his parents having relinquished their authority, he works for Philips in a menial capacity, classifying and later pressing records, and spends his spare time at the lectures and concerts organized by the Jeunesses Musicales de France. In Truffaut's case, André Bazin, whom he had first got to know while trying to run a ciné-club, was responsible for getting him out of Villejuif. Again the psychiatrist helped, and again Truffaut's parents abdicated their legal rights over their son. Bazin found him a job running film shows in factories for an organization called Travail et Culture – roughly equivalent to the

26

W.E.A., though associated particularly with the postwar activities of Resistance veterans. Truffaut then worked as a welder, and spent his spare time at the Ciné-Club du Faubourg and increasingly at the Cinémathèque. Like Antoine, he fell violently in love, went to live in a hotel opposite the home of his beloved, and spied on her comings and goings. His love was not requited. The Bazins fulfilled the role of adoptive parents for him just as Colette's parents do for Antoine. Truffaut voluntarily enlisted in the army, went absent without leave, languished in several military prisons, and was discharged – with some help from Bazin – for 'instability of character' at the age of twenty. This is also Antoine's situation at the beginning of *Baisers Volés*. From this point on the autobiographical parallels become fewer, with more divergencies than overlaps.

Bazin gave Truffaut his break as a film critic, and from 1952 Truffaut wrote regularly for *Cahiers* and *Arts*. In 1955 he made a short film, *Une Visite*, and the next year he was assistant to Roberto Rossellini, though no films came out of this period. Bazin died in 1958, too soon to see his protégé emerge, in the Sixties, as a major director. Since he began to direct, Truffaut's life was his work, and few facts, as opposed to anecdotes, are known about his private life. His marriage, from which he had two daughters, certainly gave him the chance to make *Les Mistons* and then *Les Quatre Cents Coups*. The extent to which his own marriage is revealed in *Domicile Conjugal* and *L'Amour en Fuite* is a matter for conjecture. We see Antoine Doinel's joy in paternity, his brief adultery, reconciliation with his wife and subsequent divorce. Antoine becomes a writer, and is on the verge of a new relationship at the end of the cycle. Truffaut himself divorced and later produced a third daughter, Joséphine, with Fanny Ardant, just over a year before his death.

If the autobiographical details become increasingly scattered as the Antoine Doinel cycle progresses, the psychological hints as to Truffaut's personality are even more elusive. But the following tentative hypothesis, again leaning heavily on the first two films of the cycle, may be helpful in suggesting the main lines of Truffaut's character. The danger of course lies in the temptation to equate Truffaut entirely with Antoine. The further limitations are obvious. I was present during the shooting of *Domicile Conjugal*; I have also talked to several of his friends and colleagues. Without reading too much into it, if we have accepted the parallel between the factual details of Truffaut's life and that of Antoine, perhaps it is not unreasonable to assume a measure of temperamental and psychological resemblance between the two.

The evidence afforded by the first two films in the cycle about Antoine's formative years is crucial. Gilberte is pregnant and unmarried. The father is absent, and she feels guilty and rejected. She seeks to suppress these emotions by doing away with the evidence, but her abortion attempt fails and the bastard Antoine is born. She rejects him; he is suckled by a wet-nurse and fostered by his grandmother. When he is eight, his mother is forced by his grandmother's senility to take over her parental responsibility. Meanwhile Julien Doinel, who is not Antoine's father, has married Gilberte and given her and the boy his name and respectability. But to his mother Antoine is a constant reminder of the past. Her resentment leads her to treat him with hostility, more as a domestic servant and errand boy than as a son.

By the age of thirteen Antoine has accepted this lack of maternal affection without bitterness. If he once desperately needed tenderness from his mother, he certainly no longer expects it. He is in any case becoming embarrassingly aware of his mother in another role. She is virtually the only female presence in his life, and the Oedipal urges, apparently dormant for so long, now begin to assert themselves. His mother fascinates him as a sexual creature; he is intrigued by the accoutrements of her femininity – her toilet water, eyelash curlers, perfume. She casually removes her stockings, in Truffaut's words 'that silken skin more disturbing than the real one', in Antoine's presence, as if he were immune to the sight of her bare thighs. She seems curiously unaware of the effect she has on him as he grapples with the onset of puberty and the stirrings of half-understood desires. He observes her furtively as she steps over his bed in the corridor. He overhears conversations between his parents in which sexual hints and overtones, innuendoes on themes such as working overtime and payment for services rendered, puzzle and disturb him. The images of love to which he is exposed on the cinema screen or in pin-up photographs are associated with clandestine pleasure and enjoyed in secret. Then his mother, the unattainable taboo figure, suddenly shatters his illusions about her.

Monsieur Doinel has never really been an obstacle or a rival in the classic Oedipal sense to Antoine's (mental) enjoyment of his mother

*Les Quatre Cents Coups*: 'His mother fascinates him as a sexual creature' (Claire Maurier, Albert Rémy)

— first because he is not Antoine's father, and secondly becăuse he is in any case a weak and complaisant husband. So Antoine has been free to indulge his private fantasies, in which he reigns supreme in his mother's affections. His discovery of her embracing another man in the Place Clichy has a traumatic effect on him. His idol — who is also the object of his 'pure', because unconsummated, desire — is sullied and tarnished, and in his state of shock this is not an image which his conscious mind can accept. When he returns to school next day and offers his mother's death as an excuse for his absence, the choice of parent to kill off is thus highly significant. His father is no threat, so Oedipal patricide is not called for. But his mother's attempt to cut Antoine off at birth is paralleled by his desire now to kill her off. And any guilt feelings about his repressed incestuous desire are thus also assuaged. It is the ideal solution for the severely wounded Antoine, and he grasps at it in desperation.

When it fails and Antoine is confronted with reality in the shape of his mother — very much alive — and his own imminent punishment, to be administered by his parents, his second solution, which proves equally temporary, is to run away. His English teacher's suggestion that 'perhaps it's all to do with his glands' may not be a particularly helpful comment on Antoine's struggle with the problems of puberty, but at least in so far as it contains a grain of truth our first impression that it is merely ludicrous is not quite the whole story. Antoine's adolescent crisis is further complicated by his mother's belated solicitude for his well-being and her simulated affection — based on her own self-interest — for her son as she takes him home after this escapade. Her concern here is simply to establish a complicity with Antoine to ensure that he does not reveal to his stepfather the existence of her lover. Her method is unsubtle bribery, as she attempts to discover common ground with Antoine by commiserating with him on his need to have secrets from his parents, or at least from one of them. She is again totally oblivious to the fact that Antoine's sexuality is awakened by her femininity, as she puts her arm round his shoulders, bathes him, dries him, embarrasses him by kissing his body and cuddling him. The final, incestuous touch is supplied by her insistence on tucking him up in the parental bed — Monsieur Doinel displaced at last; mother buying son's silence as a man might pay off a whore. Shortly after this feigned show of maternal affection, on their return from a happy family trip to the cinema, Julien shows off his wife's legs to Antoine, who later discovers him lustily squeezing her breasts, to her evident satisfaction.

Antoine's emotional weaning is brusquely completed by his mother when she visits him in the Reform School, the only other occasion in the film when he and his mother are together. She tells him of the unity which exists between Julien and herself, despite appearances to the contrary. From now on, as a result of Antoine's attitude, they will take no more interest in him; let him try manual work and earn his own living. The break is complete. Antoine's behaviour pattern when faced with a crisis remains consistent: he runs away. At the end of *Les Quatre Cents Coups* he is at last free — and utterly alone.

The other female influences in *Les Quatre Cents Coups* are relatively slight. The little girls seen at the puppet show and those locked up, for their own protection, by the porter at the Reform School are obviously too young. The possibility that Madame Bigey,

René's mother, could become a substitute mother for Antoine is ruled out by her chronic alcoholism and premature ageing. Antoine's curiosity is aroused by the three prostitutes locked up with him at the police station and by Pigalle at night with its strip shows, but he is too young to take his place in this world and, when he once waited for a young prostitute who was alleged to specialize in initiating young men, she never turned up. His transitory condition, midway between boyhood and manhood, is emphasized by the episode with Jeanne Moreau. As he is helping her look for her dog, his role is usurped by Jean-Claude Brialy, an older man. Antoine's contact with women remains on a fantasy level, at a distance.

There are hints that his future quest for a mother-substitute, and also an idealized, unattainable, goddess-type woman, could be temporarily satisfied by the psychiatrist at the Reform School, who combines sympathetic interest in Antoine with feminine provocation. We never see her, but by hearing her voice and seeing the effect she has on Antoine as she questions him about his intimate experiences, we recognize her as a *femme fatale* figure with maternal overtones, 'a Rubens who had read *The Second Sex*', as Truffaut says, who seduces Antoine verbally: 'You wouldn't like to stay for hours in this office?' But this potential relationship is not developed, and the psychiatrist's main role proves to be the purely practical one of helping to secure Antoine's eventual release.

If the maternal influence in Antoine's life is unsatisfactory, paternal authority is even more lacking. In the absence of Antoine's real father, Julien is a wholly inadequate substitute. He is a failure in all his roles — husband, lover (by implication), wage-earner, power-seeker, father — and he seeks escape and fulfilment in organizing car rallies. He is a complaisant cuckold who intermittently protests about his position but is not prepared to do anything to change it, just as he grumbles ineffectually about his office situation. Spasmodically he asserts arbitrary authority over Antoine, usually in the form of a brutal beating, but he has no chance of gaining Antoine's admiration or even his respect. The best he arouses is sympathy and a kind of male complicity, as if he needs Antoine as an ally in the campaign against Gilberte. This is best expressed in the scene where they prepare to eat together 'entre hommes' and Julien symbolically dons Gilberte's apron and cracks eggs interminably into a frying pan to Antoine's great amusement.

There are no strong paternal figures who might replace Julien in Antoine's esteem. The schoolmaster's reign of petty tyranny, based on a cynical system of arbitrary punishment, does no more than reinforce Antoine's sense of the injustice of the world; and the summary justice meted out by the Reform School supervisor is calculated to instil grudging submission rather than recognition of the motive behind the castigation. Not until he is sixteen and meets Colette's parents does Antoine find the 'family' he is looking for. They continue to exert a parental influence over him, reappearing in *Baisers Volés* in the guise of the Darbons, Christine's parents, who in *Domicile Conjugal* actually become Antoine's parents-in-law. One might trace the parallel with Truffaut's own need for male authority figures. First Bazin: 'He was the "just man" that you liked to be judged by, and a father to me. Even his reprimands were precious to me, for they were proof of an affectionate interest which I had been deprived of as a child.' Then perhaps also Rossellini, Hitchcock and Renoir, the last two in a professional capacity. The further working out of Antoine's search for mother substitutes, for example in the shape of Christine Darbon, and for ideal women, like Fabienne Tabard, will be taken up later.

This psychoanalytical sketch of the character of Antoine Doinel is of course incomplete in that it concentrates mainly on post-Freudian details at the expense of other factors, particularly environmental influences. I hope to redress the balance when I come to examine each film in detail. Meanwhile there is one more factor which must be taken into account, and that is the personality of Jean-Pierre Léaud and his influence on the shaping of the character of Antoine Doinel.

The first striking phenomenon to note is the duplication, with inversion of roles, of the Truffaut-Bazin relationship, with Léaud as the adoptive son. There is thus a sense of continuity in this disciple-tutor relationship, made more poignant by Bazin's death just after shooting began on *Les Quatre Cents Coups* and the dedication of the film to his memory. So Léaud, thirteen when Truffaut first met him following an advertisement in *France-Soir* and selected him for the film, was initially very much Truffaut's creation in his own image, the 'artist as a young man'. And the character of Antoine retains the essence of Truffaut's personality throughout the first two films of the cycle.

Then in *Baisers Volés*, and especially in *Domicile Conjugal*, the influence of Léaud becomes progressively more apparent. The character seems to escape from his creator and to take on a life of his own. Renoir talks of the same phenomenon, whereby a character gradually begins to reflect predominantly the actor playing the part rather than the director. Thus Antoine is less introverted, has more charm and a greater capacity to arouse sympathy in an audience than was originally anticipated by Truffaut – and these qualities are largely the contribution of Léaud. As he appears in *Domicile Conjugal*, and later in *L'Amour en Fuite*, Antoine is now a very composite character, a kind of shadowy amalgam of Truffaut and Léaud plus other influences, who, if he still displays all the habitual timidity and vulnerability of the Truffaut hero, has nevertheless veered significantly towards Léaud. Finally, as Truffaut acknowledged, his own influence on Léaud was only one of many.

At one time it seemed that Léaud was beginning to leave Antoine Doinel and François Truffaut behind, as he worked increasingly in a more committed cinema with directors like Godard and Glauber Rocha and Pasolini. But his subsequent films for Truffaut from *Les Deux Anglaises et le Continent* to *La Nuit Américaine* and finally *L'Amour en Fuite* testify to the strength of the symbiotic link between the two.

*Les Quatre Cents Coups*: Antoine at school

# 4: Les Quatre Cents Coups

However far the mature Léaud may be his own man, the adolescent Léaud in 1959 in *Les Quatre Cents Coups*, his and Truffaut's first feature, is very much moulded in the director's image. Truffaut now gives individual shape, in the person of Antoine Doinel, to his composite portrait of adolescence sketched in *Les Mistons*. The full feature length gave Truffaut scope to examine the world of the thirteen-year-old in some depth, and with the rare acuity of the adult whose memory of the same period in his own life is still raw. 'I had a fairly painful memory of my adolescence which contrasted with the regrets that others generally have for their youth ... I wanted to express this feeling that adolescence is a bad moment to get through.'

The action of the film contains very little pure invention. It is based on events which happened to Truffaut or his friends, and thus illustrates Truffaut's need in films written by him to seek authenticity by filming the real-life experiences of himself and others. His diffidence is revealed in this reluctance to rely entirely on his own creative imagination, as if the inclusion of the 'vrai' were an automatic guarantee of 'vraisemblance'. His self-confidence is further shored up by his working again with children: 'Adults inspired me with fear. Being afraid of adults, I was afraid of actors. I only felt at ease with children, with those younger than myself.' He has an instinctive affinity and sympathy with these underprivileged outsiders in the adult world.

The virtual absence of technical experiment and Truffaut's lack of interest in general theories or philosophical arguments in *Les Quatre Cents Coups*, and indeed throughout his work, result in his present position, which he describes as 'the least modern and the least intellectual of all the New Wave directors', and in his virtual abandonment by the more technique-conscious theoreticians of the New Wave. Yet as we have seen, he had never wanted to revolutionize the French cinema, merely to return to the 'good' traditions of the Thirties, represented by Vigo and particularly Renoir. Like Renoir, Truffaut uses an essentially linear narrative approach to explore the main centre of interest – the characters. And his sympathetic portrayal of people owes much to the lyrical humanism of both Renoir and the Vigo of *L'Atalante*.

As the character most often seen in close-up in *Les Quatre Cents Coups* and the focal point of the whole film, Antoine engenders a strong feeling of empathy in the audience. His central position focuses our attention on his condition and leads naturally to an attempt to analyse his behaviour. But this analysis is incomplete if it neglects to stress the environmental influences of which Antoine is a product. For the more Truffaut concentrates our attention on Antoine, the more, paradoxically, we are aware of the sociological implications of his plight. Indeed the way in which Truffaut situates his characters socially, so as to show the influence of background upon behaviour, is almost as meticulous as the detailed portraits of society produced by the author he most often quotes in his films – Honoré de Balzac. Antoine's condition could figure as a classic example of deprivation in any social worker's casebook. The step from his particular case to the general implications is an easy one, though it should be stressed that Truffaut's main aim, as outlined in several interviews, is to depict Antoine the individual rather than Antoine the symbolic spearhead of an attack on social conditions.

Truffaut's depiction of Antoine is unusually convincing on the level of verisimilitude. The authenticity of the portrait is enhanced by the quasi-documentary style of the camerawork. The restrained, unemotional treatment has the effect of inducing spontaneous sympathy in the spectator and a feeling of collective responsibility, even guilt. Antoine has not been much aware that 'Heaven lies about us in our infancy'. Rather, as 'Shades of the prison-house begin to close upon the growing boy', one would say that 'he beholds the light' or at least glimpses the sea, with its womb-like quality the symbolic goal which, once attained, should free him from his present troubles. The

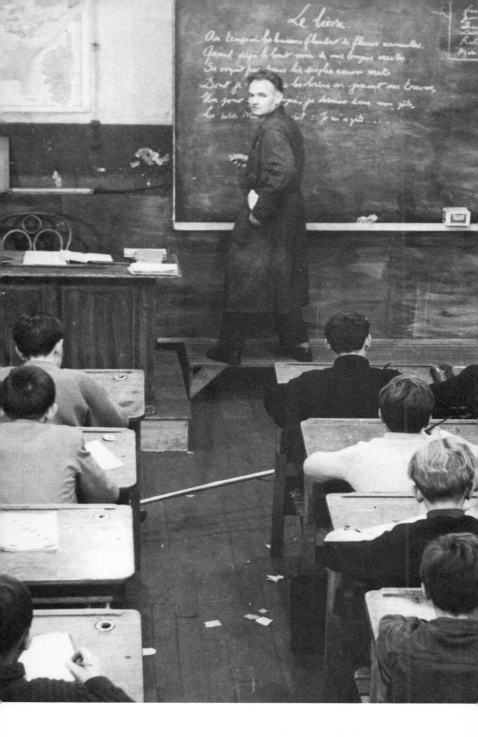

'Ludicrously incongruous love poems about hares': pedagogic practice at Antoine's school

whole film is structured round this prison/escape theme and the illusory nature of the freedom which Antoine can achieve. He proceeds in a series of picaresque adventures from one repressive institution to the next. School, family, police station, reform school, each milieu is equally inappropriate to Antoine's problems, and the adults in each setting have neither the time nor the awareness to give him the understanding he needs.

The educational system gives Antoine his first lesson in injustice. At school they are made to copy from the board, learn by heart, recite and write formal essays. Ludicrously incongruous love poems about hares, spelled out in a pedagogic voice, are rustic irrelevancies to these city toughs, and are rightly sent up by them with a rather exaggerated series of amorous sighs, wolf whistles and Marcel Marceau-type embraces round their own necks. The teacher, Petite Feuille, is the enemy who rules by force, alertness, sadism, sixth sense, sarcasm and an arbitrary system of punishment (provided a culprit is found, it doesn't matter too much who it is). The irony is quickly pointed by a shot of the Liberty, Equality, Fraternity device above the school gateway. The teacher's reign of terror is a solution of despair arising from his own bitterness and disillusionment. The nearest he gets to encouragement of his pupils is to cuff a tousle-headed boy affectionately, a gesture with latent homosexual overtones in this all-male society, reminiscent of the behaviour of the grotesque biology teacher in Vigo's *Zéro de Conduite*. His other hypocritical and pathetically inadequate reaction is seen in his attempt to change from his role of petty tyrant into that of a teacher 'in whom one should always confide' when Antoine has shocked him with his desperately improvised reason for absence, the 'death' of his mother.

On the one occasion when Antoine's imagination is fired – by reading Balzac's *A la Recherche de l'Absolu* – his attempt to reproduce the final paragraphs from memory for a class essay is unjustly treated as plagiarism and leads to his expulsion from the class. Bécassine, the other teacher glimpsed briefly, has a pronounced stammer, which gives him enough communication problems in his own language without the complications of trying to teach a second, English. The headmaster is simply a pacifier of parents.

Antoine's sense of the injustice of his punishment leads him to rebel, and his rebellion takes the form of escape from the confines of the system. Happiness is possible only when he is liberated from the prison of school and, following his friend René's example, he plays truant. At the fairground his sense of liberation, as he is whirled round on the rotor machine, with the camera tilting from his feet to his face, is an explosion of ecstasy. It also shows him alone at the centre of his emotion. René can only follow him so far; he watches Antoine here, just as later he will not be allowed in to visit him at the Reform School. Antoine is alone in all his major experiences.

The portrait of the adults and particularly of Antoine's parents in *Les Quatre Cents Coups* is harsher than Truffaut originally intended. He said that during shooting, uncertain of audience reaction, he underestimated the huge amount of sympathy there would be for Antoine and needlessly overemphasized by way of contrast the unsympathetic natures of Gilberte and Julien. He tends to compensate for this in the rest of the cycle where humanity is seen through much more rose-tinted spectacles, possibly because of the influence of his co-scriptwriters Claude de Givray and Bernard Revon. In *Les Quatre Cents Coups* the relationship between Antoine and his parents is further aggravated by their cramped living conditions. Antoine's bed is jammed in the narrow corridor of the tiny flat, and from it he overhears conversations not intended for his ears in which he is referred to dispassionately as 'le gosse', more of an organizational problem than an object of affection. He is made to do the household tasks — laying the table, stoking the boiler, running errands and emptying the oozing household refuse can — as part of his normal routine, which increases the audience's sympathy for him and hostility to his parents. Domestic disputes are the norm — sometimes arising from Gilberte's scorn for Julien prompting her extra-marital activities as a working wife in every sense of the expression, often over money matters or Gilberte's failure to do the domestic chores. The only really joyful family occasion is an isolated and spontaneous mood of hilarity which they all share as they return from a trip to the cinema.

Antoine's response to this home environment is again flight. With precocious gravity he informs his parents by letter that life with them is no longer possible, and escapes to live clandestinely at René's house after spending one night dossed down in a printing works. The central theme — that freedom is inextricably linked with isolation — is again illustrated here as Antoine walks alone past shop windows,

A rare moment of happiness *en famille*; Antoine on the run; and (*opposite*) the theft of the typewriter

some containing feminine underwear, and in the grey dawn steals a bottle of milk and gulps it down in front of a poster advertising skiing holidays – two aspects of a world which is a thousand miles from his own at this moment. He makes a token attempt to integrate with a society whose rules are incomprehensible to him, as he breaks the ice in the fountain in the Place de la Trinité and scoops a symbolic trickle of water over his face, before going back to school.

The world Antoine inhabits is as fascinating and squalid as Balzac's teeming Parisian underworld a century before. Here crime is the order of the day. Mauricet, the school sneak, steals from his parents; so does René; pockets are picked in the school cloakroom; everyone fiddles his business expenses. Antoine and René see crime as a means of achieving independence, and at the puppet show, in contrast to the bewitched wonderment and spontaneous emotion of the little children in the audience, they plan their first crime. The execution of it is left to Antoine, René sees to that. The influence of Hitchcock, noticeable before in the repeated close-ups of Antoine, is

The theme of imprisonment: Antoine at the police station and the reform school

seen again here in the way Truffaut shoots the theft of the typewriter, and later Antoine's abortive attempt to return it when they have been unable to pawn it at the Mont de Piété. The sequence with Antoine in close-up, seen from the point of view of the concierge and suddenly interrupted by a hand on his shoulder, generates suspense in a way reminiscent of the classroom scene when Antoine's parents appear in the doorway and are seen first by the teacher, with the camera then panning to a close-up of Antoine, petrified, before tracking back to show his parents.

Antoine's Paris is largely the Montmartre-Pigalle area centring on the Place Clichy, the Place de la Trinité, the steps of the Sacré Coeur – the same sleazy Paris of the prostitute, pimp and criminal, a Paris whose lights dazzle him as the police van takes him through it *en route* for the detention centre. His confinement in the police station for part of the night is little more than a restatement of the theme of his isolation from society. A succession of shots of Antoine seen through bars – in the police cell, caged in the 'chicken coop', in the police van and in the cell at the Reform School – powerfully establishes the imprisonment theme, and also ensures our total identification with Antoine's condition. The process, as he is stripped of all his belongings, put into drab uniform, photographed in two frozen poses which make him look like a sullen thug, is designed to produce a dehumanized object (an echo here of Hitchcock's *The Wrong Man*). And the regimentation to which he is now subjected is there to induce in him a state of mindless obedience, to create an acquiescent automaton who may then be reintegrated into society.

But it will take more than this to break Antoine. The urge to escape – symbolized in the film's title with its overtones not merely of punishment but also of wild liberty – is the strongest instinct he knows. René may well be blasé about the seas and oceans he has known; Antoine has never seen the sea and is therefore irresistibly drawn towards it. The final sequence of the film is much more than a homage to Vigo's *L'Atalante*, it is an encapsulation of the central theme of the bleakness of freedom once attained. This sequence is a landmark in the history of cinema. A continuous long take of Antoine running along roads is followed by a slow pan across the Seine estuary. Two successive pans show Antoine, still running through the undergrowth, then running in a shuffling hobble across the deserted sands. On the soundtrack the string accompaniment is

'The bleakness of freedom': the penultimate shot of *Les Quatre Cents Coups*

now slower and more jerky, giving way to *pizzicato* at the end. Antoine slows down as he reaches the sea, takes a few paces forward, stops and turns to face the camera. The image freezes as he looks back at us. Not one of his problems is solved, but the indictment of society is complete.

# 5: Antoine et Colette

The final cutting of the umbilical cord at the end of *Les Quatre Cents Coups* eventually leads Antoine, some three years later at the age of sixteen, to his independent, solitary status in *Antoine et Colette*. This sensitive sketch, Truffaut's contribution to the international compilation film *L'Amour à Vingt Ans* (Andrzej Wajda was another contributor), would be simply a charming, lightweight diversion if it had to stand by itself. But in the context not of the rest of the film but of the Antoine Doinel cycle as a whole this portrayal of Antoine's first fumbling contact with the opposite sex establishes him already as the diffident, vulnerable dreamer of the later films.

Predictably, after a childhood deprived of affection, Antoine's first love affair is both violent and painful. At last his vision of the ideal woman can take tangible shape; the only problem is that the dream fades away when given reality and leaves Antoine achingly unfulfilled. He now has a squalid room in the Place Clichy and works as a records classifier with Philips. His need to escape from his environment here takes a less physical form than in the previous film – he immerses himself in classical music, which provides a constant background to the film. He is attempting to remedy at least one of the inadequacies of his prematurely terminated formal education by attending all the lectures and concerts organized by the Jeunesses Musicales de France.

A flashback insert (shot for *Les Quatre Cents Coups* but not used in the final version of that film) shows Antoine and René at René's house and Monsieur Bigey's tacit connivance in Antoine's presence. This is more than Truffaut's bow to himself; it plunges the audience immediately into the emotional climate of the previous film and ensures the continuity of our sympathy for Antoine. René, always the more practical and worldly-wise, is now beginning a career in the Stock Exchange. He functions here chiefly as a sounding board for Antoine's monologues on his experiences with women. His own affair of the heart with his cousin is altogether more circumspect than Antoine's flamboyant passion, though perhaps he is less in control of his relationship than he wishes to appear, since the love letter he shows Antoine, covered in heavily lipsticked kisses, is close to the wildly romantic fantasy passions of *Les Mistons*.

Antoine succumbs to the total intoxication of first love in the Salle Pleyel, as the climax of Beethoven's 'Eroica' symphony floods over him. In a series of some forty shots Truffaut crosscuts between Antoine and Colette and the orchestra. The accelerating tempo of the music, counterpointed by the increasingly frenzied speed of the cutting, echoes Antoine's rising emotions until the final close-up of him overwhelmed by the combined force of this musical and amorous 'coup de foudre'.

A series of flashbacks, commented on by Antoine, of the three occasions when he has seen Colette, charts the love-at-a-distance phase and reveals the diffidence and timidity which are the hallmark of this typical Truffaut hero. René's advice, that with the approach work over he should now attack (again an echo of *Les Mistons* and a recurring Stendhalian theme noticeable for example in *Tirez sur le Pianiste*), ironically precedes Colette taking the initiative as she borrows Antoine's programme while he is manoeuvring for a conversational opening. Truffaut uses a commentary, spoken by an omniscient narrator, on two occasions in this film, as if the mood had not been clearly established by the visuals. On each occasion the message is ominous as far as Antoine is concerned. Colette is said to treat Antoine merely as a friend or distant cousin, and later the only advantage of Antoine's removal to the hotel opposite her home is his virtual adoption by Colette's parents rather than a newfound intimacy with the creature of his dreams.

This need to reinforce the significant moments with a verbal commentary is typical of Truffaut's reluctance to rely on the more specifically 'cinematic' ingredients at his command, and his diffidence in this respect seems a limitation here, though it contributes positively to the success of other films. In general, given a hypo-

*Antoine et Colette*: Antoine moves house

thetical choice between a word and an image, one feels that Truffaut's instinctive fondness for language would normally incline him towards the word. Sometimes, especially in *Jules et Jim* and *Les Deux Anglaises et le Continent* and also in the recital of books in *Fahrenheit 451*, because of his wish to preserve the beauty of the original language; sometimes, as in *L'Enfant Sauvage* and presumably here, because a commentary is also actually an economical and efficient technique. The impression in *Antoine et Colette* that the commentary is used simply on grounds of expediency and that it intrudes into the narrative flow might have been avoided if Truffaut had used it throughout as an integral part of the film.

Truffaut's sketch of Colette would, if developed, take its place in the long line of screen 'bitches' which fascinate him in the films of others and to which he has added in his own films, particularly in *La Sirène du Mississippi* and *Une Belle Fille Comme Moi*. In her offhand, insensitive treatment of Antoine, Colette casually exercises her power over him until she reduces him virtually to the status of an asexual object. She requires flattery, adulation, variety; he can only offer total, possessive adoration. The chasm between them is illustrated by the sequence at the cinema where Antoine, having risen to the job of actually processing records and wishing no doubt that he was the artist responsible for the song rather than the artisan who made the recording, offers Colette his first disc. Then in a repetition of the concert hall 'coup de foudre' rhythm, Truffaut crosscuts between a Movietone newsreel of a skier in the men's slalom and Antoine and Colette in the audience. He is allowed to hold her hand (no reciprocation), caress her neck and cheek (she is as cold as stone), kiss her cheek (only a gentle rebuff) but not her lips (shades of the prostitute in *Baisers Volés*); his clumsy attempt at a passionate embrace meets with a rough rejection, as the skier crunches face-first into the snow.

Antoine's emasculation as far as Colette is concerned is completed by his progressive assimilation into her family. The mother − blonde, thirty-six at most, very friendly − and the stepfather (incidentally played by François Darbon, whose name Truffaut uses for Christine's parents in the remaining films in the cycle) − a self-made man ('Education gets you nowhere') quipping, 'Take Victor Hugo, he denounced evil but never found the remedy' − provide the relaxed, affectionate background which Antoine needs. Colette's question, 'Where is one better off than in the bosom of one's family? Answer: anywhere else,' is true in the context of Truffaut's portrayal of the domestic scene elsewhere but emphatically untrue in this present context. More than being merely adoptive parents to Antoine, Colette's parents anticipate the generous portraits of humanity in *Baisers Volés* and *Domicile Conjugal*. As they turn their backs to the camera to watch television with Antoine, after Colette has just gone out with her current suitor (called Albert, a name used later for the lover-on-call in *Jules et Jim*), the image speaks eloquently of human solidarity and warmth, which is possibly a more than adequate consolation for the pains of unrequited passion. This sympathetic emphasis on friendship is an important feature in most Truffaut films, particularly of course in *Jules et Jim*, and after a gap of several years it is taken up again in the sequel to this sketch, *Baisers Volés*.

# 6: Baisers Volés

Like all the films in the Antoine Doinel cycle, *Baisers Volés* is firmly
set in the world of everyday reality. The nostalgia in the film is not
merely for things past, and particularly for Truffaut's own youth, but
also a yearning for absolutes in a world of compromise. Antoine is
not of the stuff that heroes are made, especially tragic heroes, and his
inherent romanticism and search for the perfect woman are never
sufficiently all-embracing to cause him great suffering, nor so inflex-
ible that they are incapable of moderation and adjustment to the
possible. The world may indeed be a shabby place, but it is Antoine's
world and he is at home in it. For all his charm he is a mediocrity,
inspiring in an audience not the wish to emulate him but a recognition of the ordinary man's limitations.

The same is true of the rest of the human pageant which Truffaut
parades before us, with one important qualification, which is that he
asks us to share his own indulgent, uncritical tolerance of humanity,
warts and all; a view epitomized in the euphoric death-bed discovery
of Fabienne Tabard's father that 'les gens sont formidables'. Against
this background Antoine's adventures, however closely we identify
with him, never evoke the extremes of agony or of ecstasy – sadness
and happiness, the bitter-sweet, yes; but the gamut of human
emotions over which Truffaut ranges is restricted. This framework is
both the limitation and the strength of *Baisers Volés*, and of most of
Truffaut's films. Even though he may incidentally touch on other
themes, his instinctive subject matter is the human love affair and his
strength lies in his sensitive charting of the minute fluctuations of the
heart. Whenever Truffaut senses that he might be approaching the

doom-laden passions of the Racinian universe, he sheers away, introducing a piece of comic business or a whimsical anecdote, for if his audience must not be bored neither must it be too disturbed. Whatever else he may be, Truffaut is an entertainer, a showman, and the succession of incidents and episodes in *Baisers Volés*, tenuously linked by the personality of Antoine, provides him with his ideal framework.

The Charles Trenet theme song (composed in 1943) with which the film begins and ends also supplies the title. The implication, that fleeting moments of happiness are all that may be snatched, recalls the fundamental pessimism of Thomas Hardy's view of happiness as 'but the occasional episode in a general drama of pain'. The mood of nostalgia, tender regret for faded happiness, is instantly established, though it will be subsumed in the general theme of ideals modified to a human scale. The relationship between the sexes tends to get polarized in Truffaut's world into the true love/lust dichotomy first expressed in *Les Mistons*. Between these poles is the twilight zone of compromise in which most of the couple relationships function, inside or outside marriage. Antoine's problems at either end of the scale, and in the middle, spring from his inability to recognize the limitations of each relationship and to channel his romanticism accordingly. His anachronistic behaviour in this respect, and his confusion of literature (via Balzac, Vigny or William Irish) and life, has a famous literary parallel in the disastrous adventures of Don Quixote, once his head has been turned by too much reading of the romances of chivalry.

Summoned from an atmosphere of earthy masculine camaraderie in the military prison where, incongruously, he has been reading Balzac's story of unconsummated love *Le Lys dans la Vallée*, Antoine overhears his sergeant-major giving a lecture on mine detection in which the parallels between military and sexual terminology (unexploded mines, like women, must be handled with care) again recall the language of *Les Mistons*. After his dishonourable discharge from the army, at the age of about twenty-one, he asserts his masculinity by rushing off, still in uniform, to the nearest prostitute. His air of being in a hurry, casually whistling to feign the confidence he does not feel and the experience he does not have, falters when it is obvious that he is not familiar with the procedure of paying on entry, and collapses entirely in the face of the extreme functionalism of the

Innocence and experience: Antoine learns the rules of the game in *Baisers Volés*

sex on offer. The prostitute refuses his aggressive kiss (never with the customers), moves away when he tries to stroke her hair ('I've just lacquered it'), and disengages herself from his attempt to stroke her breasts and remove her sweater ('I'll keep it on, I've had bronchitis'). When she prepares to wash him, Antoine's ardour is cooled, and his nerve and will fail. This clinical detachment is too far from the emotional involvement he needs and – misguidedly – expects.

Rushing downstairs, as always in moments of panic or embarrassment, he encounters a second prostitute arranging the next meeting with a regular client, and she seems to offer the affection he wants. Truffaut here uses a recurring device for indicating sexual desire – a shot of a woman's legs from the point of view of a man following her upstairs. Antoine, despite his uniform, is no longer in the army, so her quip about his being in the artillery and her liking for big guns has an ironical ring. The third episode with a prostitute, much later in the film, reveals Antoine's increased experience. He now pays the prostitute at once and does not expect her to remove all her clothes or prolong the encounter. This new attitude can also be seen as an assertion of life in the face of death, sex as an antidote to neurotic despair, for this encounter immediately follows the funeral of Monsieur Henri, his colleague at the detective agency, whose Bazin-like paternal guidance is thus brusquely cut off. Antoine's reaction has been anticipated by the possibly fictitious account provided by another colleague, Paul, of his love-making with a cousin in an attic on the day of a family funeral: 'After a death making love is a way of compensating . . . one needs to prove one exists.'

This same search for identity, the need to reassure himself of his own existence, is arguably at the base of Antoine's earlier posturing in front of a mirror, repeating aloud with varying intensity his own name and the names of the two major feminine influences in his life, Fabienne Tabard and Christine Darbon. The potentially comical consequences of trying to learn a foreign language exclusively by this method of repeating aloud are developed in *Domicile Conjugal*: a clear echo of Truffaut's own frustrating experience with the sounds of the English language. Antoine's spectacular incompetence in each of his jobs – hotel receptionist, private detective, TV repair man – scarcely equips him to find fulfilment in the role-playing and professional pride which might be associated with any one of them – unlike Monsieur Henri, for instance, with his amusingly stubborn memory for details of past cases and his recommendation, based on experience, of a good restaurant for salt pork and lentils.

Nor is Antoine convincing in his ego-boosting accounts of his sexual prowess with a very tall girl ('the walls trembled'), which he relates to Paul, who is himself conducting an unsatisfying liaison with Catherine, controlled by her and marked by furtive embraces in the office washroom. Other characters, such as the vague acquaintance found rummaging in street litter bins who announces that his script is about to be accepted for television, also fall short of the images of themselves they hope to present to the world. Albert and Colette of *Antoine et Colette*, now married with a child, embarrassingly fail to make contact with Antoine during a chance encounter. Truffaut exploits all these relationships for laughter; but behind the gags one senses the sadness.

Throughout the film there is a recurring emphasis on the role of chance in life. This emphasis, as we have seen, is admirably suited to the loose episodic structure into which Truffaut can introduce at

The search for identity: Antoine alone

random casual contacts and fleeting encounters. Chance operates as an important factor at key moments in Antoine's life. It is because he happens to hear of a job as night porter that he meets Monsieur Henri, becomes a private detective and so happens to encounter Fabienne Tabard. Later a similar casual sequence leads from his chance encounter with Monsieur Darbon in a motor accident to his being the man who turns up in response to Christine's summons to repair the family television set, whence his progress into bed and then into marriage with Christine. The stranger who observes and plans and tries to shape his destiny ends up empty-handed and alone. Chance, and the extent to which life is based on chance, not choice, is central to *Baisers Volés*, as it is to *Tirez sur le Pianiste*, *La Sirène du Mississippi* and *La Femme d'à Côté*.

The mask and the face, the mirage and the reality, is a motif Truffaut brings out again and again in *Baisers Volés*. The film's most subtly grotesque comic portrait is that of Monsieur Tabard, the shoe-shop proprietor. His deadpan, unconscious self-revelation in an

The vulnerable male: Monsieur Tabard (Michel Lonsdale) in his shoe shop

interview with Monsieur Blady, the head of the detective agency, together with his unawareness of the gap between his mask and his real self, is a masterpiece of sustained humour. The solemn mask proclaims that its owner has no problems, is wonderfully married to a 'superior' woman, is without racial prejudice and doesn't need friends. Underneath is revealed the vulnerable male with a strong fear of being cuckolded, no sense of humour, lecherous and with a persecution complex and fascist tendencies.

The embodiment of ideal womanhood in the shape of Fabienne Tabard (Delphine Seyrig, exuding unapproachable mystery), dream goddess and fairytale princess, is Antoine's Damascus road vision, inspiring in him awed veneration and complete enslavement. This image of beatific purity and mystic inner radiance is made for worship: 'She is not a woman, she is an apparition.' His incredulity when it appears that she has a lover (in fact himself) and is therefore corruptible is based on his certainty that 'this woman is far above such a thing'. Similarly, the homosexual's refusal to believe that his

'She is not a woman, she is an apparition': Delphine Seyrig as Fabienne Tabard

'friend' is now married and has a child demonstrates that Antoine is not the only dreamer who needs to idolize his beloved. Truffaut's treatment of the homosexual as a source of laughter is a good example of the film's insistence on amusement at all costs. Truffaut's intentionally comic guying of the man's petulant reaction to the truth about his lover raises an easy laugh. But this parody of the gullible lover finds an echo, as we shall see, in the declaration of permanent love by the ubiquitous stranger at the end of the film — at which point Truffaut's attitude is at least ambiguous.

The miniature love idyll between Antoine and Fabienne is highlighted by three fixing shots of the Sacré Coeur seen at different times of the day from Antoine's window in the Square d'Anvers. These shots, recalling Monet's paintings of Rouen cathedral in different lights, not only establish the chronology of events but also contribute to the emotional effect of the scenes they encompass. Antoine writes his letter of farewell to Fabienne in the best romantic tradition, referring to the 'impossibility of sentiments between them' as between Félix and Madame de Mortsauf in *Le Lys dans la Vallée*, his voice heard against a shot of the Sacré Coeur by night. The letter is sent by *pneumatique*, the Parisian system of sending express letters by underground pipeline, and its progress is followed through the sewer complex in images of unexpected beauty. Prefaced by an early morning shot of the Sacré Coeur and a municipal street water-cart, then a track to the façade of Antoine's flat, framing his window in an impressionistic, grainy-textured frozen shot, Fabienne's reply is — herself. Antoine, like Charlie in *Tirez sur le Pianiste*, is seen in bed looking like a little boy whose eyes are popping out of his head. Dismissing unconsummated love as pathetic, Fabienne with tact and delicacy reveals herself as a woman, the opposite of an apparition, exceptional and unique just as every other woman is. Antoine accepts her proposal that they spend a few hours together and then, whatever happens, never see each other again in order to preserve the exceptional quality of the relationship. Perfection in human affairs is possible only as an isolated interlude. We next see the Sacré Coeur in broad daylight, and in the shot three people whose presence menaces this fragile and transient happiness.

A more intractable type of hopeless passion is represented by the mysterious stranger in the white raincoat who appears, accompanied by his own sinister theme music, at intervals throughout the film. The way he follows Christine and spies on her is reminiscent of Antoine's behaviour in *Antoine et Colette*, which in turn, as Truffaut has admitted, was based on his own experience as a young man. A further interesting parallel, between cinema-going and voyeurism, is of course not one which Truffaut is the first to draw, but he has described how in his adolescence seeing a film was always a furtive, clandestine activity – often because he was playing truant from school or sneaking out of the house without his parents' permission. The camera as voyeur aspect is most apparent in *Baisers Volés* in the delightful sequence in Christine's house just before the end. The camera lingers in close-up along a trail of assorted television components scattered on the floor, slowly mounts the stairs (almost step by step), peeps tantalizingly into the wrong bedroom, and finally glances into the right one to reveal (gentle anti-climax) Antoine and Christine discreetly in bed. Truffaut has playfully mocked the voyeurism in us all.

The build-up to this scene is echoed in the rhythm of the final episode with the enigmatic stranger. Is the man's voyeuristic behaviour no longer a substitute for action, and does the suspense music indicate a violent climax? Not so, since Truffaut seems again to be playing, Hitchcock-style, on audience expectation. Or is he? Perhaps he could not really cope with the character, and having created him he now has to dispose of him. So he makes him deliver to Christine an incongruously solemn declaration of his eternal, 'definitive' love for her, which she predictably rejects as 'completely mad'. But the scene is doubly disturbing. Truffaut seems at this point to be injecting a note of irony, even of self-mockery, in this sidelong view of an attitude which is uncomfortably close to the aspirations of Antoine and thus of Truffaut himself. Truffaut's own nostalgia for the purity and innocence of an absolute love shows through in the scene – such a love as may be dreamed about but not attained outside the world of courtly romance.

The reality of romance is typified by the compromise affair between Antoine and Christine. Initially Christine has been for Antoine an idealized outlet for love by correspondence (cf. the anecdote on the same theme in *Jules et Jim*) until his discharge from the army. Then she takes the initiative. When they meet for the first time after his discharge, he moves as if to shake hands with her but she kisses him. She invites him to her house, provocatively invites a kiss in the

Absolute love and the reality of romance: Delphine Seyrig and (*below*) Antoine and Christine (Claude Jade) on the way to 'domicile conjugal'

cellar and seems momentarily surprised when Antoine, roused, pins her roughly against the wall, like a whore. She constantly pursues him, and in the 'dépit amoureux' scene in the park it is she who provokes their provisional break-up; although during this squabble Antoine, 'dazed by Fabienne', has proclaimed that love must be based on admiration and respect, whereas he has never felt more than friendship for Christine. Finally, she engineers his seduction, and the film ends with the implication that their life together, and their problems, are about to begin.

The human contact of the detective agency can be seen as a step in Antoine's search for a substitute family; but with Christine's parents as his future in-laws, he need look no further for the warmth and affection he enjoys at their house. And Christine herself, temporarily eclipsed by the divine power of Fabienne, is an acceptable human compromise, who offers domestic peace, comradeship and an affectionate, 'maternal' indulgence of Antoine's whims.

# 7: Domicile Conjugal

This penultimate chapter in the Antoine Doinel cycle was shot in 1970, two years after *Baisers Volés* and preceded by *La Sirène du Mississippi* and *L'Enfant Sauvage*, which to some extent reiterates the themes launched in *Les Quatre Cents Coups*. There are signs in this chapter that Truffaut had perhaps overworked this particular vein, and had not avoided the danger of repetition, with variations on what looked like developing into the Jean-Pierre Léaud formula comedy.

On a first viewing the temptation is to dismiss *Domicile Conjugal* as trivial — pleasant enough, but lightweight and with no real force. Truffaut tries so hard to entertain. The gags come not singlehanded, as in *Baisers Volés*, but in battalions, with at least one gag per sequence, selected by Truffaut from the mass of tape-recorded interviews with concierges, bistro owners, flower sellers and so on, assembled by his co-scriptwriters Claude de Givray and Bernard Revon. Life is a merry romp; people are still 'fantastic', only more so. The human types who live around the courtyard where much of the action takes place (recalling the use Renoir makes of a similar setting in *Le Crime de Monsieur Lange*) are larger-than-life caricatures whose function is to entertain. Unfortunately, they tend to enter on cue for jokey dialogue in carefully contrived 'chance' encounters. The illusion of spontaneity created in *Baisers Volés* seems to have been lost in this self-conscious manipulation of walk-on parts.

At this stage one does not expect socio-political comment from Truffaut. In *Baisers Volés*, filmed among the barricades and tear gas of the events of May 1968, he simply made fleeting allusions to the replacement of Henri Langlois as director of the Paris Cinémathèque, the demonstrations and the police violence.* So two years later it is hardly surprising that in *Domicile Conjugal* political allusions to France under Pompidou should be even more anodyne. The concierge talks about the 'dustbins of the new society'; a 'politicized' prostitute complains that her trade falls off after the middle of the month because her customers have no money left; most pointed of all is Léaud's superb timing and deadpan expression as he reads aloud from Antoine's letter to a senator thanking him for his influence in enabling him to obtain a telephone in one week 'whereas the average Frenchman has been requesting one for years'. But in general the film comes perilously close to the French situation comedy with no teeth, which Truffaut used to pan as a critic. After thus isolating, Godard-style, the 'con' in *Domicile Conjugal*, what then remains?

First, the film is a considerable success as a comedy in its own right. If a few jokes inevitably fall flat or seem contrived, most of them are right on cue, thanks usually to the inspired timing of Léaud, an instinctively 'cinematic' animal equally at home with the visual demands of mime and the verbal comedy of the anecdote. It is no gratuitous homage to Tati that shows a Monsieur Hulot character in the Métro as a train arrives: Tati has said that he sees Hulot in restaurants, at airports, everywhere but in films. So Truffaut takes him at his word and uses his own best double here. In the preface to *Les Aventures d'Antoine Doinel*, which contains the scripts of the first four films in the cycle, Truffaut describes how he himself was once mistaken for Léaud/Doinel by a café owner, and he seems to be claiming a similar ubiquity for the character to that of the Hulot of *Playtime*, the world of which is specifically evoked in the American sequences of *Domicile Conjugal*.

---

* Despite Truffaut's personal involvement in the battle, as co-treasurer of the committee for the defence of the Cinémathèque, was at pains in interviews on the subject to emphasize that this was in no way for him a generalized political commitment, but simply a way of repaying a personal debt to Langlois for his own cinematic education. Truffaut's interest was confined to ensuring that Langlois was reinstated at the Cinémathèque so that cinephiles should again be able to immerse themselves in the extraordinary range of films shown there, just as Truffaut and his colleagues had done in the Fifties.

*Domicile Conjugal*: the road to domesticity

At its best, the humour works on several levels. In one sequence in the Métro, Antoine walks in front of an advertising poster for 'Bébé Confort'. The camera remains on the poster (the audience, though not Antoine, is already aware that Christine is consulting a gynaecologist) as Antoine, expressionless as Buster Keaton, walks out of the frame for a second, then suddenly returns and looks at the poster of a smiling baby. As he tries to rush out of the station (he always runs when in a panic), he is trapped by an automatic door closing – just as he is trapped in his father-to-be situation. The implications are allowed to sink in as he stares at the baby in close-up.

During the mistaken identity interview with the boss of the American company, Monsieur Max, Antoine's toneless incantation of set phrases memorized from his linguaphone course in spoken English is cumulatively and explosively comic. His technique of using the one word he understands as a springboard for a sentence produces a wildly surreal situation unsurpassed by Ionesco. Monsieur Max: 'Do you read American newspapers?' Antoine: 'I prefer poetry to prose . . .' Monsieur Max: 'Do you have a car?' Antoine: 'I am not in a hurry, I prefer to cross the town.' Monsieur Max shows Antoine the company grounds from the window – 'It's impressive, isn't it?' Antoine: 'The birds fly high in the sky . . .' Finally Monsieur Max makes his little joke: 'The employees of my company are so pleased here, they are sad if they have to stay at home on Sundays.' (We laugh.) Antoine (serious): 'Really!' But the interest of this episode is not limited to its humour. Antoine has reached his present fluency (about Truffaut's own level) via stammered English lessons in *Les Quatre Cents Coups* and a record course in *Baisers Volés*, by which he hoped to emulate his idol, Fabienne; so there is a continuity with the other films in the cycle. Much more than this, language plays an important part in *Domicile Conjugal*, and is a recurring pre-occupation of Truffaut elsewhere, particularly in *Fahrenheit 451* and *L'Enfant Sauvage*. Without language, the implication is, there is minimal communication and therefore impoverished human relationships; and it is this factor which is responsible for the early collapse of Antoine's affair with Kyoko, the exotic Japanese girl (this film's version of Antoine's inscrutable woman), and his speedy return to Christine and the comfortable familiarity of their native idiom.

Comedy of character, and situation comedy of a slightly more predictable kind, arises from the cross-section of humanity in the courtyard. The range is wide, even if the subjects are sometimes a shade contrived: from a gentle smile at the eccentric Great War veteran who refuses to go out until Marshal Pétain's remains are buried at Verdun, to disbelieving laughter at the boldness of the bistrot *patron's* conspiratorial, nymphomaniac wife who attempts to seduce a stubbornly uninterested Antoine: 'You, I want you, I'll have you!' The 'strangler', as a sinister neighbour is called behind his back, provides an element of suspense, which Truffaut seems to think is a necessary ingredient in any film; though often, as here, it is superfluous, even as an indication of the volatility of public opinion, when the strangler is revealed as a television female impersonator and attitudes change from hostility to admiration. False trails leading nowhere are part of Truffaut's legacy from Hitchcock, but audience manipulation as an end in itself is a pretty barren exercise and Truffaut's use of it is unnecessary.

An altogether more intriguing phenomenon is the way Truffaut blurs the distinctions between cinema and life. In this film, apart from the Hulot character, there is the television impersonation of Delphine Seyrig, first speaking a mélange of lines from Resnais' *L'Année Dernière à Marienbad*, not all of which were spoken by her in the film, then delivering her Fabienne Tabard speech in *Baisers Volés* – about being not an apparition but a woman – and agreeing that she *is* exceptional. Christine laughs, but Antoine is disconcerted – and so are we. This merging of an actor's previous roles in films made by Truffaut and by others produces a composite screen image of the actor which is confusing enough in itself, though it may well be close to the vague public image of the star as the combined essence of all the film parts (s)he has played. Even so, Truffaut, unlike for instance Godard, does not normally employ alienation techniques, the object of which is to distance us from the film, hinder facile identification with the character, and make us aware that we are in the cinema. On the contrary, a working principle valid for all his films has been that what is happening on the screen (with very rare exceptions, such as parts of *Tirez sur le Pianiste* and the dreamlike flashbacks in *La Mariée était en noir*) represents 'reality'. Though his definition of that reality is fairly elastic – elastic enough, for instance, to contain films within films, plugs for friends' films, copies of key scenes from films which influenced him, and a plethora of allusions in the form of verbal or visual quotations.

Access to Truffaut's inner cinematic world is obviously limited. To participate totally in the self-preening experience and the thrill of recognition when an allusion is picked up or an in-joke clicks, it is necessary to *be* Truffaut and to have experienced the years of intensive exposure to films which make him the total product of the cinema that he is. Virtually the whole of his education took place at the cinema and his saturation in the medium is absolute; his claim 'Je suis cinéma' is no exaggeration. The specialist cinephile has the next best chance of penetrating this world. But what of the 'general public, who enter the cinema by chance after looking at the stills outside'? And what of Truffaut's much vaunted claim to be a non-intellectual whose films have a very wide appeal ('I work for the public of the Cinéac Saint-Lazare, for the spectator who drifts in casually to watch a bit of film before catching his train')? Well, this spectator will miss most of the references. But perhaps after all he will not be missing very much, since fortunately these references do not constitute an essential part of any Truffaut film, more a gilding of the lily; and provided the spectator is responsive to the emotional turmoil of people in love, he will be capable of grasping the essence of Truffaut.

The other major redeeming feature of *Domicile Conjugal*, apart from the comedy, is the delicacy and sensitivity with which Truffaut 'illumines the commonplace' and transforms the elements of daily life into something like a fairytale. While retaining all his habitual *pudeur*, he still achieves the frankness of an intimate confession. His method at its best is always understatement and suggestion rather than open demonstration.

The opening sequence, framing Christine's legs in close-up as the camera tracks lovingly behind her while she does her shopping and pertly corrects traders who call her 'Mademoiselle', is not just expository. It also establishes her as a sexual object now within marriage, and therefore inaccessible, except to the voyeuristic gaze of the camera (and the audience) and that of lecherous old men, such as the parking attendant who 'given the chance would not say no'. Needless to say, as usual Truffaut does not exploit the erotic possibilities; as in *Jules et Jim*, the only nakedness we shall see is that of the emotions. Whatever effect she has on other men, Christine does not exactly inspire overwhelming desire in Antoine. His peremptory peck when they meet, before rushing downstairs to the important business of dyeing carnations, reminds us that this *is* a marriage and that for Truffaut, along with La Rochefoucauld, 'There may be good marriages, but there are no delightful ones.'

Not that the nymphomaniac Ginette, with her direct frontal assault, is a threat to the couple. Antoine may lack initiative, but extreme blatancy merely intimidates him. Likewise at the brothel he is embarrassed by the overwhelming selection of whores paraded before him, and he needs to personalize the relationship with the one to whom he is eventually led, telling her that she is especially beautiful and kissing her hand as he leaves.

As the marriage deteriorates, the whole basis for its existence begins to seem insubstantial. Antoine, having missed out on the maternal tenderness phase in childhood, needs to compensate for it now; he needs to receive more affection and indulgence than he is able, or prepared, to give. By marrying Christine, a typically well-brought-up girl of the petite bourgeoisie (the sort that has always

67

'Bed . . . is mainly a place for talking and reading' (Claude Jade, Jean-Pierre Léaud)

attracted him, according to his ex-colleague from the television repair firm), Antoine admits to being in love not just with her but with the whole family – a kind of package deal which ensures that he will be surrounded by a comfortable, protective framework. He will have fitful moments of tenderness for Christine and will sometimes amuse and entertain her, but she will rarely be more than the audience of one in front of whom his ego flowers. Bed, for Antoine and Christine, is mainly a place for talking and reading. Antoine is initially so bashful that he tells Christine not to look while he undresses and then leaps into bed with his pyjama trousers on. Christine has not developed beyond the adolescent stage of love at a distance, and idolizes Nureyev, symbol of masculinity. Together they are like little children playing at marriage. In this context the birth of their son Alphonse is a minor miracle.

Even so, it is not as an escape from a loveless marriage that Antoine is driven to writing. His inclination (vocation would be too positive a word) has always been towards solitary self-expression, and

A minor miracle: Antoine, Christine and Alphonse

at key moments in his life he has always been alone. His solitude is especially acute when his paternal pride, as he poses for photographs of himself with the baby in the maternity ward, is deflated by Christine's telling him to leave (she too has felt alone in pregnancy). Antoine walks the streets, as in *Les Quatre Cents Coups*, unable to share his joyful news with anyone. He telephones a friend, who is not in; he meets a casual acquaintance, who profits from the occasion to borrow more money from him and whose 'merde' is the only emotional response Antoine will get that night to his declaration that he is 'fou de joie'. The loneliness sub-theme in *Domicile Conjugal* includes also the hotchpotch of characters who make fleeting contact in the courtyard or in the bistrot, and whose conversation is typified by the monologue delivered by Césarin, the bistrot owner, along well-worn tracks to an audience of one (a sewer worker) who isn't even listening and in fact drifts off while Césarin is still talking.

Antoine's explosion of passion for Kyoko, the Japanese girl who visits the American firm where he works (or rather plays) at tele-guiding model boats in a miniature harbour simulation, is little more than a restatement of the adoration of pure womanhood theme, personified by Fabienne Tabard in *Baisers Volés*. Again the initiative is taken by the woman. She gets Antoine alone with her; she drops her bracelet in the pool, thus ensuring a future rendezvous; she kisses Antoine when he is about to shake hands; she gives him the illusion of choosing how they spend the evening, but in fact she has it planned; she invites him to come again soon by writing on bits of paper folded inside wax flowers – 'Viens quand tu peux, mais peux bientôt' (lines spoken by Catherine, that other male-devouring goddess, in *Jules et Jim*). She is, according to Antoine, more exceptional even than other women because she is 'another continent' (he studies the theme in his bedtime reading), a fact which Christine fails to appreciate. But Antoine has difficulty in showing enthusiasm for Kyoko's unsmiling declaration that he is the man she would most like to commit suicide with, and the charms of exoticism begin to pale.

Already Antoine and Christine have progressed from sleeping separately to actually living separately. Their intimacy never included much sharing of unpalatable truths about each other, and Truffaut now captures this by intercutting a 'confidential' conversation between Antoine and Monique, the secretary at the office, with one between Christine and her neighbour Sylvana, the doting wife of the time-obsessed tenor whose voice periodically rings out across the courtyard. Even these 'conversations' are not much more than two people delivering monologues. Unlike Monique, who would 'marry a lamp-post if it conversed with me', Antoine reveals that he does not detest solitude, that he had been at first amused, then moved, by the hyper-politeness of the socially superior Christine, and that now he sees her as a little girl pretending to be a woman. Christine, for her part a virgin when they married, was afraid of men and also afraid of losing Antoine. Sylvana, who has previously been seen by Christine as a threat, with her 'beautiful bosom and voluptuous mouth', knows that 'all men are children' and advocates patience, for Antoine will return. Her assertion that 'life is fantastic', whereas the disillusioned Christine finds it merely 'disgusting', recalls the *Baisers Volés* theme of 'les gens sont formidables'. It also has a ring of irony in Sylvana's mouth, since on every occasion we have seen her she has been engaged in a frantic, losing race against the clock, trying to dress and

'Another continent': Antoine and the inscrutable Orient

catch up with her impatient husband, for whom, as the omniscient recluse informs us, 'time is time'.

The film's rather flimsy ending in fact takes up this theme. One year later, Antoine is back in the conjugal nest, pacing up and down and flinging Christine's bag and coat downstairs in a somewhat contrived repetition of the gestures of Sylvana's husband. Whereupon Sylvana gushingly exclaims that 'at last they love each other', which elicits from her husband three successive expressions – scepticism, wryness and mock anger – each frozen in close-up. With this, Truffaut's traditional 'ambiguous happy ending', the film closes.

Before this, though, there has been evidence of the possibility at least of survival for Antoine and Christine's relationship, in their relative honesty and tenderness at one point when they meet at the flat, drawn by their mutual consideration for Alphonse. Truffaut seems to be pointing to a limitation of his own work when Christine says pointedly about Antoine's novel, 'I don't like this idea of relating one's youth, criticizing one's parents, soiling them. A work of art can't be a settling of accounts.' Antoine's confession that he and Kyoko no longer know what to say to each other is a way of ensuring Christine's sympathetic complicity, and a preparation for her role as confidante when he telephones her three times during his interminable meal with Kyoko, complaining of his boredom, saying he wants to escape, and finding renewed tenderness in a telephone embrace with his wife. Most moving and saddening of all is Antoine's previous declaration of love and Christine's response, because it says everything about what their relationship is and what it is not:

Antoine: You are my little sister, you are my daughter, you are my mother.
Christine: I should also like to have been your wife.

# 8: L'Amour en Fuite

There are seven films and eight years between *Domicile Conjugal* and *L'Amour en Fuite*, the final episode in the Antoine Doinel cycle, shot in 1978. Truffaut had long pondered the possibility of this final sequence, which would allow him to exploit the valuable footage left over from the previous Doinel films in fascinating new combinations. Above all his homage to Jean-Pierre Léaud would now be complete in this portrayal of his evolution over a period of some twenty years, a similar time span incidentally to that of the triangular love affair in *Jules et Jim*.

*L'Amour en Fuite* again raises the question of the relationship between art and life, which also figured prominently in *La Nuit Américaine*. Is cinema more important than life? To Truffaut it *is* life so the question does not really arise. But in *La Nuit Américaine*, while coming down on the side of cinema, he still spends the major part of the film demonstrating the way in which the fiction of the film permeates the facts of the actors' lives, so that ultimately it proves impossible to distinguish between them.

The issue is further blurred by the strength of the autobiographical element in all his films. As the publicity for *L'Amour en Fuite* makes clear, 'Antoine Doinel . . . is neither François Truffaut nor Jean-Pierre Léaud. He is an imaginary screen character situated somewhere between the two.' Truffaut with his celebrated hostility to the documentary genre is certainly not seeking here to depict an autobiographically authentic version of a period of his own life. Nor is he seeking to document, home-movie style, Léaud's progression from adolescence to the brink of 'maturity'. To claim

73

Colette (Marie-France Pisier) and Sabine (Dorothée) in 'L'Amour en Fuite'

otherwise would be to underplay the fictional and narrative dimensions, which are so crucial to Truffaut's conception of cinema. Truffaut's reply to the charge of opportunism and expediency in his re-use of pre-shot footage is to point out that this material amounts to less than a fifth of the final version. But the fact remains that this is still quite a substantial proportion and the viewer perhaps needs to share the director's fascination with Léaud's evolution to accept this defence without demur.

Truffaut can be accused of self-indulgence in the pleasure he appears to take in wilfully confusing the spectator with Léaud's screen persona in this film, just as with Delphine Seyrig in *Domicile Conjugal*. Thus flashbacks featuring Léaud in the earlier Doinel

Antoine (Jean-Pierre Léaud) and Sabine (Dorothée) 'pretend their relationship is for life!'

films in the role of Antoine are interspersed with extracts from *La Nuit Américaine*, where Léaud plays the part of Alphonse and is involved in a relationship with Liliane. The impression created is that all these episodes are part of the same cycle, whereas in fact the only unifying factor is the presence of Léaud in both films. Truffaut attempts to bridge the gap between the two films by shooting some extra footage of Léaud and Liliane (Dani) for this film but he merely succeeds in adding to the confusion created by the blurring of the gap between the two roles.

A further intriguing dimension for fans of the Antoine Doinel cycle is afforded in the course of the film by Antoine's rearrangement of key episodes from the earlier films for the purposes of the novel which he has written based upon his own life and experiences. The device is of course a highly convenient way of allowing Truffaut to use the pre-shot footage as flashback material throughout the film. Antoine's novel then provides a commentary on this material, sometimes leading to a wilful distortion of events. So in his novel, for example, Antoine states that it was Colette's family that moved house to live opposite him, whereas in fact in *Antoine et Colette* the move happened the other way round as Antoine sought to be close to Colette. Another layer is added by having Colette reappear in *L'Amour en Fuite* and enabling her to provide a gloss on Antoine's fictionalized account by depicting her reading Antoine's novel. This potentially intriguing device never actually develops into a comment on the creative process – the fact that all artistic creations use reality as raw material, that so-called objective documentaries are always angled in line with the view of the presenter or the choices made by the writer/director and so on. But Truffaut never really pursues any of these themes and one is left with his rather perfunctory, throwaway treatment which is at best light-hearted in a nudge-nudge sort of way and at worst downright irritating and frustrating. The charge is not so much that he chooses not to explore an interesting dimension in a particular way but rather that, after arousing expectations, he is seen merely to be gratuitously playing around.

The main interest of this lightweight film lies in the fact that it is the final link in the Antoine Doinel chain. What happens to the hero in this ultimate sequence, described by Truffaut as 'a recapitulation, a patchwork mosaic and the conclusion to the cycle', provides what Truffaut has called a 'relatively happy' ending, when the flimsy new couple agree that, even if their relationship cannot be for life, they can at least 'pretend that it is'.

Truffaut said that out of all the films in the Antoine Doinel cycle his preference was for the *Antoine et Colette* episode, possibly one suspects because of the importance to him in his own life of the 'Colette' figure and her rejection of him. If, as Brassens says, 'one never forgets the first girl one takes in one's arms', then it is also true that one never forgets one's first rejection. The crucial comment on Antoine, who is shown in flashback at the ages of thirteen, nineteen, twenty-four and twenty-eight, and in the present film aged thirty-three, applies to him at all stages of his existence.

It is made by Liliane and is an echo from both *Domicile Conjugal* and *La Nuit Américaine*: 'He needs a wife, mistress, little sister and wetnurse all in one and I feel incapable of playing all those parts.' Antoine in *L'Amour en Fuite* is always in a hurry, snatching at love 'on the run', as the title suggests, just as in *Baisers Volés* he stole whatever love came his way. He is marked by his painful adolescence – *Les 400 Coups*; unrequited love – *Antoine et Colette*; infatuation with a married woman before settling for security – *Baisers Volés*; marriage and infidelity – *Domicile Conjugal*; and finally by divorce in *L'Amour en Fuite*. The film in fact opens with Antoine and Christine obtaining a divorce 'by mutual consent' thus making French legal history. In the course of the story Antoine is briefly in contact with three of the key women from previous Léaud films – Colette, who is now a lawyer, Christine and Liliane. But with the exception of Colette they are little more than a series of fleeting episodes, linking with Antoine's past but hardly central to this film. Their function is to allow Antoine – and ourselves – to relive moments of his past and sometimes to see them in a new light. Colette at least has the merit of consistency. She said no fourteen years before and, despite Truffaut's toying with the spectators' expectations, she finally says no again. Antoine, pausing only to adjust his amour propre, is soon off on a more tantalising pursuit. Meanwhile by chance, and this is typical of Truffaut, he meets the man who was his mother's devoted lover for many years and who gives Antoine a truer picture of her. There follows a painful period as Antoine relives the bad moments in the Doinel cycle which led him to equate the image of woman-as-whore with his own mother. Further flashbacks from *Une Belle Fille Comme Moi*, *La Nuit Américaine* and *L'Homme qui aimait les Femmes* reinforce this image. Finally in the scene in the cemetery, when Antoine and his mother's lover visit her tomb, there is a feeling that now, at last and too late, he is capable of the understanding and forgiveness that could have led to a reconciliation. Interviews with Truffaut have revealed a parallel evolution in his relationship with his mother, who died in 1968. Meanwhile back in the main plot Antoine has finally pieced together the jigsaw puzzle that has led him to Sabine, a salesgirl in a record shop, who believes that love is a two-way process involving sharing and sacrifices. As their life together begins, with the title music emphasising the need to grab love while you can on the soundtrack, the film reaches its typically open ending. Though quite how much optimism is justified for the future of this couple, when half of it consists of the child/man Antoine/Léaud/Truffaut, is anyone's guess.

# 9: Tirez sur le Pianiste

*Tirez sur le Pianiste* takes us back eighteen years to resume the chronological thread interrupted by the Antoine Doinel cycle. The transition is not as abrupt as it seems. Despite the fact that Truffaut's second feature is an adaptation of an American novel (*Down There* by David Goodis), it is as much a vehicle for personal expression of his recurring themes as any of the more obviously individual statements in the Doinel films. From the point of view of the film's overall tone, however, with its affectionate comic pastiche of the Hollywood B-feature and its deliberate playing on audience reaction, it can perhaps best be appreciated in the historical context of the New Wave. A helpful yardstick for comparison might be Godard's *A Bout de Souffle*, with its similar blend of melodrama, jokiness and love story and its capacity for swerving off in unexpected directions. The total effect of *Tirez sur le Pianiste* is achieved by an unlikely mixture of genres and moods which, against all the odds, results in a quirky, offbeat masterpiece ahead of its time. The essence is elusive; the effect is invigorating.

Truffaut, whose criteria for judging his own films tended to be overly influenced by their box-office performance, rated *Tirez sur le Pianiste* as a failure simply because it did not enjoy great popular success. Yet many would see it as his most idiosyncratic work and wish he had continued in the same vein. Truffaut criticized the very qualities of 'self-indulgence' and 'self-assurance' which are the film's stengths and give it its freewheeling exuberance and bite. For once he believed in himself and had the courage to make the film he wanted to make: not exactly without regard to audience reaction, but rather with the deliberate intention of frequently disorienting and misleading his audience, Hitchcock-fashion. The film was made in the winter of 1959, in the afterglow of the dramatically unexpected success of *Les Quatre Cents Coups*, and Truffaut's change of direction, as often happens with a director's second film, was striking. The film's appeal is particularly to the sophisticated cinephile, that is to a minority audience. Truffaut was so disillusioned by the poor financial returns that he never again risked such bold experiment or allowed himself such untrammelled freedom.

Truffaut's first feature-length adaptation (Marcel Moussy collaborated on the script) from a literary source must obviously be judged as a film in its own right. But it is important in passing to compare it with the Goodis novel. Truffaut selects details of characterization, notably in the person of the pianist – Eddie in the novel, Charlie Kohler in the film* – according to his own criteria for male 'heroes'. He avoids, for instance, any mention of Charlie's hereditary violent streak in his 'wild man' past, just as he neglects much of the hard-bitten poetry of the novel. Yet he retains such aspects of the original as Charlie's sexual timidity and wish for non-involvement, perfectly captured by the inspired device of using as soundtrack at key points Charlie's 'stream of consciousness' monologue, delivered in a fast, self-mocking monotone, and gently spoofing the melodramatic commentary of many a Hollywood gangster film (as Godard did in *Alphaville* with the character of Lemmy Caution, secret agent). Given the transposition of the setting from America to France – and particularly from Harriet's Hut in downtown Philadelphia, where the novel's hero is 'a two-bit piano player without a past', to the sleazy Parisian bistrot where Charlie plays – Truffaut is remarkably faithful to the atmosphere and climate of the original, and also to the general framework and even many of the incidents. Again, the influence of the American films which Truffaut and the *Cahiers* critics saw after the war is clearly visible in this evocation of the idea of America as filtered through the B-films of the period.

After the opening close-up of the inside of a piano with the hammers pounding out the insistently rhythmic and melancholy theme tune, the first sequence plunges us at once into the atmosphere

---

* To avoid confusion I refer to him as Charlie throughout, even after the revelation of his real name in the flashback sequence.

*Tirez sur le Pianiste*: the influence of the Hollywood B-film (Serge Davri, Charles Aznavour)

of the gangster chase. A man is running at night down a dimly lit street, pursued by a car with dazzling headlights and screaming tyres. Suddenly he slumps to the ground – hit by the car, or perhaps riddled with bullets. Actually, he has run into a lamp-post. Our instinctive identification with the victim and our acceptance of the chase scene at face value have been mocked. This is only a spoof of the Hollywood production-line thrillers which formed Truffaut's staple film diet in post-war Paris. The action is then suspended as a complete stranger comes up, helps the man to his feet, and begins to recount his marriage – how he once thought of getting rid of his wife, but then two years after his marriage fell in love with her. A comic insert; scepticism about marriage; 'les gens sont formidables' again: familiar Truffaut attitudes all. The two men part. Then the first man, remembering he is in a gangster film, runs off again at breakneck speed as the narrative thread is resumed.

The next sequence, in the bistrot where the man seeks asylum, packs in a lot of information and concludes the exposition. The man's brother, Edouard, greets him laconically: 'Call me Charlie and wait there.' Charlie's role-playing is even more conscious than that of other Truffaut heroes. He does not want to know about the pursuing gangsters, double-crossed by a brother he has not seen for years. The affectionate reference to the Marx brothers – this brother is called Chico, there are four brothers in all – is the first of many cinematic in-jokes and allusions in the film. The introduction of the middle-aged bouncer barman, Plyne (Goodis' Harleyville Hugger, who 'has it bad for the waitress', who in her turn is 'strictly solo – she wants no part of any man'), shows his pathetic attempt to assert his authority – to play out *his* role – by threatening Chico, who is loudly informing the customers that his brother, Charlie, should be in a concert hall and not in this dump. Plyne is coldly deflated by Charlie, who rejects his familiarity: 'Call me *Mister* Kohler.'

Charlie thumps out mechanical rhythms at the piano, while the attitudes of the people dancing before his neutral gaze constitute an amusing microcosm of sexual behaviour. Chico attempts a cheerfully blatant pick-up ('You are very desirable. That's why I desire you') and proposes marriage. A generously endowed woman, disconcerted by her small dancing partner's frank interest in her bosom, is told not to worry because he is a doctor. And the comic patter is reinforced by the visual demonstration of the sex theme, as Clarisse, the archetypal

'Mechanical rhythms': Charlie at the piano

big-hearted prostitute, amuses herself by temporarily deserting her role as a plaything of the customers and performing a comic dance with a little man whom she alternately playfully entices towards her and then physically repels, the whole performance watched by two connoisseurs of form whose simulated world-weariness ill conceals their own inexperience. All good, jokey fun, with Truffaut's habitual serious undertones, until the chase is resumed with the sudden arrival of the two gangsters, comic cut-out uglies of laughable inefficiency. Their efforts are easily foiled by Charlie, jerked from his inner reverie and thus involved by chance, despite his desire for isolation, in the affairs of others.

A shot of the singer, frantically jigging up and down as he delivers at amazing speed – in an effort to distract attention from the man-hunt in progress – a song about Avanie and Framboise being the teats of destiny, shows his bobbing head juxtaposed in the frame with the faces of Victor, the constantly grinning drummer, and Charlie, looking deadpan and gloomy. The gap between public performance and

'The persistent melancholy of Charlie's character and situation' (Charles Aznavour)

private reality is succinctly revealed. The shot also announces the persistent melancholy of Charlie's character and situation, which tends to get lost among the film's plethora of snappy comic effects. Plyne is revealed as simply a wreck, further down the human scrapheap than Charlie but engaged in an equally painful identity quest. In this he is hampered by limited perceptiveness and infantile illusions about the world and women, which result in a disastrous inability to make contact with anyone, including Charlie, whose soured lucidity and self-containment insulate him in an equally sterile existence. Charlie offers only mockery in return for Plyne's admiration of him and his power to attract the waitress, Léna. He rebuffs Plyne's friendship-seeking lament about being unattractive to women with the usual Truffaut flippancy that it may be gland trouble (a remark made about Antoine in *Les Quatre Cents Coups*), and takes jokingly the suggestion that his own problem is timidity; though the idea intrigues him enough for him to repeat to himself 'I am afraid' in a semi-mocking, quizzical tone which debunks Plyne, amuses the audience and suggests his vulnerability despite his smokescreen, all at the same time.

The poignant woodwind theme which Truffaut often uses for its emotional effect and especially to highlight a gentle 'true love' scene is heard now as Léna, taking the initiative, waits for Charlie, borrows money from him and asks him to see her home. The mood anticipated by the music is enhanced by the soundtrack (Charlie's inner monologue as he rehearses subtle ways of asking her for a drink, finally blurts out a direct proposal, and finds she has slipped away) and brilliantly emphasized by the camerawork: medium close-ups of the couple's head and shoulders, then a series of close-ups at waist level from the rear, stressing Charlie's tentative hand movements behind Léna's back as, fists clenched, he plans his campaign and, Julien Sorel-style, begins to count on his fingers. Truffaut's use here of the camera's capacity to create a mood, in this case humour, prefigures a similar example in *Baisers Volés*. We see a rear view of a woman's head in close-up, then a shot of her head and shoulders, then the camera pulls back to a medium long-shot of the woman with Antoine walking beside her – revealing what it has previously concealed, not merely that she is not alone but that she is taller than Antoine by at least a head. The significance of Antoine's earlier interest in special techniques for very tall girls becomes clear.

85

Charlie's wry acceptance of the comic anti-climax of his man-oeuvres – 'Perhaps it was better that way' – indicates a man more accustomed to the consolations of stoical resignation than confident of his sexual prowess. The film, not for the first time, then swerves off in an unexpected direction as Charlie switches off the emotional intensity which exposes his vulnerability and enjoys a relaxed, uncomplicated, quipping sexual encounter with his neighbour Clarisse, the prostitute, in which audience involvement is again deliberately shattered by a distancing device. Truffaut mildly upbraids the arbitrary prudery of the censor, and also reminds us that we are in the cinema, as Charlie covers Clarisse's breasts with a sheet and says, 'At the cinema it's always like that.'

The reappearance of the gangsters (Ernest and Momo) next morning, heralded by a burst of melodramatic suspense music, points up again their role as comic characters, as Fido, Charlie's younger brother, bombs their car windscreen from on high with a carton of milk – another example of the consciously incongruous interpolation of gratuitous humour into an otherwise plausible love story, and typical of the film's abrupt switches of tone.

The ensuing abortive abduction of Charlie, then Léna, by the crooks, with Ernest twirling his revolver and trying to act tough (he has seen too many gangster films), offers scope for another burlesque spoof on the theme of sex. First a split-screen triple iris shot shows Plyne in three consecutive stages of betraying Charlie and Léna to the crooks, another Truffaut homage to the silent screen and in particular to Abel Gance. Then, in a pastiche of standard demonstrations of twisted criminal motivation, Momo reveals his life's quest for revenge on all women because one of them inadvertently caused the death of his father, knocked down by a car as he stared at her in the street. The sexual frenzy into which Ernest and Momo work themselves merely by talking about women as sexual objects who 'only want one thing, but expect to be spoken to as well' is temporarily interrupted by Charlie, quoting a familiar Truffaut comic maxim (used also in *La Mariée était en noir*): 'When you've seen one, you've seen them all.' Their obsession with women's clothing designed to attract men, particularly underwear and stockings, verges on fetishism, and establishes these gangsters firmly in the mainstream tradition of the Truffaut male victim.

Léna and Charlie escape, and his awareness of the danger of

falling – metaphorically as well as literally – if he looks at her legs as she precedes him upstairs to her room provides the run-in to the extended flashback sequence introduced by Léna's 'Formerly it was different'. The idyll of Charlie and his wife Thérésa in bed together is disturbed by the superimposition of an iris shot of the evil impresario Lars Schmeel; the shot, interposed between the couple, is soon faded out, but it leaves an impression of menace, like a fairytale ogre. Three shots, in progressively increasing close-up (and accompanied by a disorienting long-shot), of Charlie's finger nervously approaching the bell-push at Schmeel's door illustrate what Schmeel calls his 'illness' of timidity. The impresario later tries to eliminate this flaw in his protégé's public image by subjecting him to a course in personality projection, at the end of which Charlie resembles the required posturing stereotype (foreshadowing Antoine's mouthing of dis-connected English phrases in *Domicile Conjugal*), though his real identity remains resolutely enigmatic. His career as an international pianist, pounding out the classics in the world's concert halls, produces in him both total egocentricity and at the same time doubt about his talent, and puts intolerable strain on his marriage. A sad near-embrace at the end of one sequence fades out, suggesting per-haps that the couple are doomed not to complete it. And when Thérésa's burden of guilt drives her to talk to Charlie, it is too late.

Thérésa's confession is prefaced by an ominous silence on the soundtrack. The camera crosscuts between husband and wife, then pans from face to face as she spells out the details of the love or lust dilemma involved in her sacrifice of herself to Schmeel in furtherance of Charlie's career. Charlie's tortured inner monologue reflects his own dilemma: his realization of the need to go to Thérésa and comfort her and his inability to do so. He walks out, hesitates, runs back; but the message implied in the increasingly urgent tension of the music is confirmed as the camera seems to rush past him into the room and on to the balcony, and plunges giddily down to reveal Thérésa's body on the pavement below – followed, as in *Les Mistons*, by a shot of newspaper headlines announcing the tragedy. Léna's voice then takes the narrative up to the present, and the image fades from a poster of Edouard Saroyan, concert pianist, to a succession of superimposed embraces between Léna and Charlie in bed, whose tenderness, heightened by the death scene and its accompanying sense of loss, is also reminiscent of *Les Mistons*.

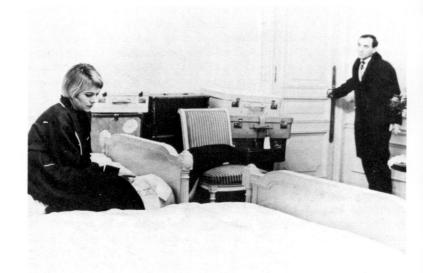

Isolation: Charlie and Thérésa (Nicole Berger)

But even at this time of burgeoning love, the danger signs are there to remind us that in Truffaut's world happiness is transient. Léna takes over Charlie, organizing him into going out to buy her a pair of stockings (the same fate befalls Pierre in *La Peau Douce*) and trying to resuscitate his sense of identity by telling him to resume his career and his real name. She counters the nihilism of his 'Pourquoi?' with the pragmatism of her 'Pour qui?', but realistically asks him to have the courage to tell her when he no longer loves her. Then the comic kidnapping (comic in action, but with serious consequences) of Fido by the gangsters, and their naïve attempts, like little boys, to impress him with their musical cigarette lighters, new snorkel pens, alligator belts and other toys, allows Truffaut a moment of joyfully gratuitous farce, unthinkable in any other film, as one of the gangsters swears on the head of his mother and an iris insert shows a little old lady keeling over stricken, legs in the air.

Typically, the climax of the film – the confrontation between Plyne, Charlie and Léna – is placed within this comic sequence.

Intervention: Charlie tackles Plyne

Charlie's solitude is threatened, despite Léna's view that 'even when he's with somebody he is alone'. He tries his usual remedy of immersing himself in his music as Léna demolishes Plyne and his pretensions to masculinity. Charlie muses, 'Even now, when she's calling him names, he can't take his eyes off her. She's overdoing it, but what can I tell her? That Plyne isn't as bad as she paints him? He's a poor slob who hoped to be somebody and didn't make it.' Forced to intervene to save Léna, Charlie is exposed to the full violence of Plyne's anger and sudden disillusionment that this woman, his idol, has been 'sullied' and that she no longer conforms to his ideal. 'Woman is pure, delicate, fragile; woman is supreme, magical,' he informs Charlie, gripping him tightly round the throat in a last desperate effort to assert his masculinity, and refusing Charlie's peace offer (in what might almost be an alternative ending to *Baisers Volés*, with Plyne as the stranger and Charlie as Antoine). Charlie, on the point of choking to death, finds his discarded knife and, as in Hitchcock's *Dial M for Murder*, stabs Plyne, aiming for his arm but

'At last, after many adventures . . .': Charlie and Léna (Marie Dubois) on the run

accidentally killing him – the culmination of the note of fatalism which runs through the film. Plyne's concept of the purity of woman, though expressed in this incongruous context, is in the best tradition of declarations by dying gangsters; and also of Truffaut's misunderstood heroes.

'At last, after many adventures' (for this is a kind of fairy story), including Charlie's rescue by Léna and their escape by car, the setting changes from the lights of the city to the blinding snow of the Alps. During the journey a singer on the car radio has proclaimed, 'When I don't love you any more, I'll wear my cap,' a somewhat unsubtle touch to remind us that this *may* be a fairy story but that it is also set in a world where love ends. Charlie, 'despite himself, despite herself', sends Léna away and joins his brothers, Richard and Chico, in their hideout – actually the parental home, from which the parents have been banished.

The final gun battle with the gangsters, prefaced by a combination of the woodwind theme and the gangsters' own suspense music followed by an ominous silence, and by Léna's return to take Charlie back, epitomizes the disturbing clash of tones which has characterized the film. First, comedy – the ease with which Fido escapes from the crooks as they slip on the ice; then burlesque of the gangster film's traditional finale – gun butts shatter windows, one of the gangsters twirls his gun again, but it still looks like a toy gun. We have been manipulated into identifying with Charlie and Léna. We have been willing a happy ending, ignoring the carefully planted omens of tragedy – the song, the suspense music, the gun. The crosscutting between Léna, Charlie and the gangsters has given us the scent of danger. But the continuing aura of comedy surrounding the gangsters has cushioned us in our expectation that the situation cannot be unhappily resolved. Then suddenly Léna is hit by a bullet, and in an agonizingly prolonged shot her body slides down the slope, insistently proclaiming the reality, and the finality, of this moment. A briefly frozen close-up of her face confirms that Charlie need not have bothered to run frantically to her. Another Truffaut idyll is over, destroyed by chance.

Charlie returns to his piano in the bar. He pounds out the haunting theme, and his bleak, mournful stare as the intensity of the music increases gives way to the opening shot of the piano hammers. The circle is complete. There is a new waitress in the bar; but Charlie's solitude is unassailable and his nihilism intact. The attractive possibility that the film might at any moment lurch in a new direction has been preserved until the end. This capacity to surprise (and mislead) the audience is what distinguishes this from every other Truffaut film. True, anything might *happen* in a loose, episodic structure such as that of *Baisers Volés*. But it is the unexpected switching of *moods* which gives *Tirez sur le Pianiste* its particular, elusive quality.

# 10: Jules et Jim

*Tirez sur le Pianiste* is the kind of film Truffaut might have gone on making if he had chosen to risk all on working out his talent for manipulating genres and moods – allusions to French cinema, echoes of America and Hollywood B-film clichés – into excitingly fresh permutations in French settings. Godard went on to do something like this. But *Tirez sur le Pianiste* is Truffaut's only contribution to this early Sixties, characteristically New Wave style of film-making; and his three other films based on American sources have little of the same exuberant experimentation. Yet if *Tirez sur le Pianiste* is the key testament to Truffaut's American inclinations, his next film is an even greater achievement in the mainstream of what might be termed the French lyrical tradition.

A hymn to total freedom in love and a lament for the impossibility of achieving it, *Jules et Jim* is Truffaut's third feature; which, by his own criteria, makes it his first 'definitive' film and the beginning of his mature work. Despite the potentially scandalous nature of the subject (even in 1961) – two men and a woman sharing life and love over a period of twenty years – Truffaut's film successfully reproduces the essential purity of the source novel, a first work by Henri-Pierre Roché, written in 1953 when the author was seventy-four.

Almost the whole of the novel is there, but with incidents rearranged and some different emphases, notably in connection with the role of Catherine, which is a composite portrait combining predominantly the personality of the novel's Kathe with the qualities of many of the other women who appear in the first part of the book.

The spirit and tone of the original, particularly its adult fairytale quality, are miraculously preserved. The actual text figures either as dialogue – occasionally transposed to different speakers or situations – or as part of the ubiquitous commentary, spoken unobtrusively but tellingly as a poetic, ironic accompaniment to the film. Truffaut has made the masculine friendship aspect secondary to the central emphasis on the dominance of Catherine, and to this extent the title is more appropriate to the novel than to the film. The failure of the heterosexual couple is the major theme of the film, together with the corollary that all other solutions, including the *ménage à trois*, are equally doomed.

In both the book and the film it is the passionate pursuit of happiness and the satisfaction of their transient desires which provide the characters with their reasons for living. In their preoccupation with personal happiness they are representative of the bohemian intellectuals and free-thinkers of the café society of the period between 1912 and the early 1930s. The ravages of the First World War and later the public book-burning by the Nazis are background episodes which temporarily interrupt but do not divert them from the dilettante activities and whimsical humour of their own lives.

The fairytale opening commentary, quickly spoken in a neutral tone, describes how in pre-war Paris a friendship blossomed between the small, fair-haired Jules from 'somewhere in Central Europe' and the tall, thin Frenchman, Jim. They are soon inseparable, sharing a love of language and literature and a relative indifference towards money. 'So they talked easily, each finding in the other the best listener of his life.' The first major difference between them is in their experience with women. 'There were no women in Jules' life in Paris, and he wanted one. In Jim's life there were several.' Jim introduces his friend to a number of women, with whom Jules is 'a little bit in love for a week' (thus telescoping incidentally several early chapters of the novel). Finally, 'against Jim's advice, Jules turns to the professionals . . . but without finding satisfaction there.' The whole of the exposition has been a series of rapid, silent scenes showing the two men alone or with women, counterpointed by the affectionate commentary, like a story being read aloud.

A gentle dig at anarchists who can't spell serves as a pretext to introduce Thérèse, who picks up any man prepared to offer her a bed for the night. She is the embodiment of existential freedom. Her allegiance is to herself and to the mood of the moment, captured perfectly by her giddy imitation of a steam engine, with the camera panning after her in close-up as she puffs round the room with smoke pouring from the wrong end of the lighted cigarette in her mouth, and the music zooming along in harmony. The same routine serves later to attract another man, and Jules, guilty of neglecting her because he is immersed in conversation with Jim, ruefully declares that he wasn't in love with her: 'For me she was my young mother and my attentive daughter both at the same time.' Shades of Antoine Doinel, and the first hint of Jules' vulnerability and gentleness, as well as a foretaste of the future havoc to be wrought by a more imperiously demanding woman.

Jim meanwhile has been conducting his own experiment in carefully circumscribed freedom with Gilberte. His jealous guarding of this freedom, on the grounds that living together for any length of time would make their relationship indistinguishable from marriage, illustrates *his* need rather than hers, and in this respect sharply differentiates him from Jules. Individual freedom and happiness is again limited by rules in a gently amusing incident later in the café. Jules sketches on a round table-top the face of a woman he has loved. 'Jim wanted to buy the table,' the commentary tells us, 'but it was not possible – the proprietor would only sell all the twelve tables together.' But the atmosphere of the fairytale in which everything is possible soon takes over again. The two friends are captivated by a lantern slide of an ancient statue – a calmly smiling woman's face. They resolve to go and see it together and set off immediately for an island in the Adriatic, where they are struck dumb by the statue's beauty. The contrast here between the transience of human affairs and the permanence of art recalls some lines in Keats' 'Ode on a Grecian Urn' ('Thou, silent form, dost tease us out of thought/As doth eternity ... Thou shalt remain, in midst of other woe/Than ours ...'). 'Had they ever met that smile before? Never. What would they do if they met it one day? They would follow it.' Thus begins their worship of the goddess by whom, according to the traditions of classical mythology, they will be ultimately and inexorably destroyed.

A series of close-ups of the eyes, mouth, nose, chin and forehead of Catherine, whose smile recalls that of the statue, heralds the entrance of this personification of the deity, while the subsequent

*Jules et Jim*: 'Thomas always wins' (Jeanne Moreau, Henri Serre, Oskar Werner)

narrowing of the screen to frame her and Jules radiating happiness together indicates the designation of her first victim. Jules' suffering begins as he first dimly perceives the threat posed by Catherine to their idyllic masculine friendship, and the spectre of rivalry between them in his 'Not this one, Jim, eh?' Later, the success of the masculine disguise by which Catherine becomes 'Thomas' moves them 'as if by a symbol, which they did not understand'. Significantly, Thomas always wins, even if, as in the race between the three of them, by cheating a little. Her extremism may be the result of her mixed aristocratic and peasant parentage. It is her decision that the three of them should leave for the seaside; and their departure is prefaced by her ceremonial burning of letters from past lovers, which almost leads to her accidental self-immolation – another hint of mortality. Her passionate attachment to vitriol as a weapon to throw in men's lying eyes is an unhappy omen for any man who dares to spurn her.

The dazzling Mediterranean light, in the shot of them all peering at

Triangles: the transient happiness of a golden moment

the dawn from separate windows of their white house by the sea, reflects the optimism of this golden moment. But implicit in this mood is an awareness of the fragility of their happiness and the impermanence of people dwarfed by the permanence of nature and the eternities. So in a wood near the shore, to the accompaniment of the joyful strings and woodwind theme, they search for 'the last traces of civilization', symbolized by odd pieces of junk, remnants of the old order from which they are trying to escape. The camera, panning across the treetops from Jim's vantage point, reinforces the possibility of happiness in a retreat to nature, but then we come down to earth again with Jim's warning to Jules that Catherine within the bounds of marriage will never be happy on this earth: 'She is an apparition for all to appreciate perhaps, but not a woman for any one man' (a view which reflects Antoine's image of Fabienne in *Baisers Volés*). But this does not preclude the possibility of bursts of happiness, expressed most typically when the three swoop along on bicycles on a winding road, sometimes apart, sometimes side by

Catherine centre-stage: 'She wants to be free. She invents her life, every moment.'

side, Catherine often speeding ahead, in a visual anticipation of the permutations of their future fluctuating relationship.

Catherine's gigantic ego is happy only at the centre of things. When she is neglected, she draws attention to herself again by slapping Jules' face hard. They laugh, after an uneasy pause; and Catherine, centre stage again, is seen in a series of close-ups, each momentarily frozen, illustrating the gamut of emotions through which she has passed. Back in Paris again, Catherine's identification with the heroine of the play they have just seen ('She wants to be free. She invents her life, every moment') isolates her from the two men, who become absorbed in their own discussion. Here Truffaut puts one of his favourite comic lines into Catherine's mouth ('Men only think of one thing'), and Jules caps it with a jesting, 'Exactly, Madame, we men only ever think about one thing – and you encourage us.' Catherine's characteristic response is a melodramatic jump into the Seine, accompanied by increasingly sinister music, which frightens and silences him (with reason, as the film's penultimate

97

sequence makes clear). The whole sequence is shot at night, reflecting the despondency of the mood at this point.

One of the key factors in the film's success, which one begins to appreciate about this point, is the quality of the performances, and particularly that of Jeanne Moreau. Truffaut's frequent tributes in interviews to her exceptional professionalism have been echoed by other directors. His claim that she is the only woman known to him who combines the 'masculine' virtues of camaraderie and strength with totally captivating feminine charm seems an understatement in the context of this film. The part is so much the actress, and vice versa, that it seems inconceivable that any other actress could have played it. Moreau outshines both Oskar Werner (Jules) and Henri Serre (Jim), and that is no fault of their fine, sympathetic performances.

Catherine misses a rendezvous with Jim in the café (she has, of course, little sense of time and less of obligation), and this gives Truffaut the opportunity to introduce one of his stock types – 'I never make jokes ... moreover I have no sense of humour' – anticipating the roles (played by Michel Lonsdale) of Monsieur Tabard in *Baisers Volés* and the sententious politician Morane in *La Mariée était en noir*. Jules announces that he is to marry Catherine, and the mood of merriment as he boisterously bellows out the 'Marseillaise' in an increasingly strong Austrian accent gives way to pathos as the image dissolves first to a poster announcing general mobilization, then to actual newsreel footage of the Great War (some of it stretched to fit the Scope frame, and so incidentally conveying an impression of war as grotesque). Personal concerns, however, remain uppermost. Jules writes passionately to Catherine from the trenches, and each man is afraid of accidentally killing the other. Then, 'Jules' country had lost the war, Jim's had won it. But the real victory was that they were alive – both of them . . .'

When the trio meet after the war in the chalet on the Rhine where Jules and Catherine are living, Jim's feelings for Catherine can only be channelled through her little daughter Sabine, with whom on one occasion he rolls over and over in the grass. Sabine already imitates her mother's intonations and gestures, a *femme fatale* in embryo. Throughout the film the passage of time is reflected only in externals – a chronological procession of Picassos, Catherine's clothes, and near the end her wearing of spectacles – but the characters do not age physically and their emotional turmoil does not diminish with time. The sense of timelessness, and also the evanescence of time, is never far from the centre of *Jules et Jim.*

Jim's self-contained independence as a roving freelance journalist, 'un curieux' who can live anywhere, gives him a freedom limited only by the need to meet copy deadlines. Jules, as a biologist writer, gradually retreats into monastic seclusion, rejected by Catherine as a husband 'I am not the man she needs, and she is not the kind of woman to put up with it.' His qualities of 'generosity, innocence, vulnerability and indulgence' (anticipating Louis in *La Sirène du Mississippi*), which in Catherine's words once dazzled and conquered her and set him apart from other men, are now tolerable to her only in doses prescribed by her, and interspersed with her absences with other lovers. Jules' plight is paralleled by the anecdote of the young gunner deflowered by correspondence, his successful wooing of the girl he wrote to from the trenches, culminating in his passionate declaration, 'Your breasts are the only bombs I know,' followed by his death in hospital on the eve of the armistice.

The rest of the film is haunted by Catherine's theme song about the whirlwind of life in which a couple are flung together, then apart, in an endlessly repeated cycle until finally they embrace for ever. Jules' altruistic self-effacement ('If you love her, stop thinking of me as an obstacle') is the prelude to the first real embrace between Jim and Catherine, seen – as in *Les Mistons* – in profile, with Jim reverently touching Catherine's forehead, nose and mouth as gently as the camera which caressed these same features of the goddess on her first appearance. 'Their first kiss lasted the rest of the night. When Jim got up, he was enslaved. Other women no longer existed for him.'

Yet Catherine's expression – 'full of curiosity and an extraordinary jubilation' – is not incompatible with her view that 'one is never completely in love for more than a moment'. Once Jim has become a fixture in the chalet, she is able to undertake the seduction of Jules in the same spirit of scientific curiosity. Jim's understanding of her attitude (as he later tells Gilberte, 'Once Catherine wants to do something, so long as she thinks that it won't hurt anyone else – she can be mistaken of course – she does it, for her own enjoyment and to learn something from it. That way she hopes to become wise') does not preclude his jealousy, captured visually by a crane shot from outside the chalet looking in first at Jim on the ground floor, zooming

'An endlessly repeated cycle': Catherine, Jules and Jim at the Rhine chalet

up to Jules and Catherine above romping on the bed, then back to Jim pacing up and down.

Recalled briefly to Paris by his newspaper, Jim encounters the unstoppable Thérèse, who breathlessly and hilariously recounts her whirlwind romantic exploits, in which her own ego has been the constant driving force. A contrasting aspect of sexuality is provided by the silent Denise, introduced to Jim by her 'owner' as 'a beautiful object ... sex in its pure state'. Having postponed his return to Catherine, whom he is to marry, because he wants to avoid hurting Gilberte, Jim finds when he does finally return that Catherine, true to her eye for an eye philosophy, is otherwise engaged. Jules and Jim are equalized as courtiers whose role is to pay homage to their (absent) queen.

Catherine unexpectedly returns, and Jim and she spend a night of trembling chastity. Another idyllic period begins. An aerial shot of the chalet and surrounding woods, taken from a helicopter, is echoed in the soaring music: 'The promised land was in sight.' Then, as the camera pulls away from the chalet, 'The promised land suddenly retreated.' Jim and Catherine's inability to produce children drives her into Jules' paternal embrace, and Jim returns to Paris after one last pitiful hotel encounter with Catherine, when 'they took each other once more, without knowing why, perhaps as a kind of full stop. It was like a burial, or as if they were already dead.' (In general, the chance of happiness in *Jules et Jim* always seems most likely in an outdoor setting – on the beach, in the meadows and forests. It tends to recede in the more confining interiors – the chalet, the hotel room, the house near Paris: an observation pinpointed by the film's strongly contrasted black and white photography.) Another aerial view of woodland, with Catherine's face superimposed on it, hints tantalizingly at the possibility of happiness offered by Catherine's news of her pregnancy. As Jim, finally convinced after a frustrating exchange of letters, prepares to respond to Catherine's summons, 'Viens quand tu peux, mais peux bientôt' (Roché's formula, used also, as we have seen, by Kyoko in *Domicile Conjugal*), the child dies in the womb and with it all further hope. 'Thus between the two of them they had created nothing.'

In an atmosphere of gathering gloom (nature again echoing emotion), a chance meeting between Jules and Jim leads to a car drive with Catherine, during which she still plays out her former role by abandoning the two men in favour of a night with Albert, one of her earlier lovers and a shadowy presence in the second half of the film. Jim's resistance to Catherine's last impassioned plea for love, and his lucid account of the reasons for the failure of their relationship ('Like you, I think that, in love, the couple is not ideal . . . You wanted to construct something better, refusing hypocrisy and resignation. You wanted to invent love from the beginning . . . but pioneers should be humble, without egoism'), is too much for Catherine. Truffaut's melodramatic treatment of her immediate attempt to shoot Jim is one of the few jarring moments in the film.

Jim's respite is shortlived. A few months later, in full view of Jules, Catherine's triumph is complete. In a repeat performance of her leap into the Seine, the rhythm of the editing equally fast, she is smiling inscrutably (the statue again) as with Jim beside her she drives her car over a ruined bridge into the water. Her last existential choice is made. Stark close-ups of coffins consumed by flames in the crematorium, and of grinding machinery and levers, echo the earlier

'In an atmosphere of gathering gloom': Jim and Catherine together for the last time

shots of dials and gear levers in Catherine's car, and emphasize the astonishingly swift and inevitable reduction of people to ashes. 'They left nothing behind them,' is the commentary's epitaph.

Catherine had sown chaos in Jules' life until he was sick of it. A feeling of relief swept over him. His friendship with Jim had no equivalent in love.' The rules of society thwart Jules' wish to mingle the ashes and scatter them to the wind from the top of a hill . . . 'It was not allowed.' Alone at the end, he walks downhill accompanied by Catherine's voice on the soundtrack singing about the whirlwind of life.

Existential choice: Catherine on her way to Albert; Jules with the ashes

# 11: La Peau Douce

At first sight it may seem surprising that Truffaut should have chosen to elaborate on the triangle theme so soon after his apparently exhaustive treatment of it in *Jules et Jim* (though in fact two years separate the films, with the *Antoine et Colette* sketch intervening). Perhaps it was the possibility of introducing very different emphases within the same overall triangular framework that induced him to make another variation on the theme. The *Jules et Jim* triangle had a strong woman at the apex and two men at the base, the whole trio being linked by friendship. *La Peau Douce* has a weak man at the apex and at the base two women who never meet; so the relationships in the film are always based on the couple – Pierre and wife, or Pierre and mistress. What is distinctive in this film about the cinematically hackneyed subject of adultery is the treatment, the style and the tone which Truffaut brings to it. His originality in *La Peau Douce* lies in his extraordinary capacity to combine severely restrained, impartial observation of his characters with a real sympathy and sensitivity to their problems. His tolerance, embracing Renoir's view that everyone always has his reasons, implies also a refusal to judge. Truffaut's concern with detailed but neutral observation discourages identification with any one character and, as in the Antoine Doinel cycle, prompts a feeling of sympathy tinged with sadness for their not uncommon circumstances.

In contrast with *Jules et Jim* there is very little of the fairytale about the unpoetical realism of *La Peau Douce*, and no nostalgic period charm to be exploited in the strictly contemporary settings – Paris, Lisbon, Rheims and Orly airport. Truffaut's original script, written in collaboration with Jean-Louis Richard, consists largely of everyday dialogue of an intentional banality. The role of language here is mainly to conceal emotion rather than to convey it. Inner passions and tensions are portrayed visually: the close-up, over which the opening credits are superimposed, of the clasping and unclasping of two hands – a woman's and a man's wearing a wedding ring – is eloquent of the film's general emphasis on impermanence and infidelity. Similarly the anxieties and pressures which weigh on Pierre Lachenay throughout the film are clearly indicated in the first sequence, which shows him emerging at speed from the Métro, looking for a taxi, forced to wait until the lights change before crossing a road, hurrying out of the lift, fumbling for the keys to his flat and finally being forced to ring for his wife Franca to let him in. From the outset Pierre hardly stops moving.

The reason for his haste – his plane for Lisbon, where he is to lecture on Balzac, leaves in forty minutes – is now spelled out, and the tension created by this piece of information (how well Truffaut learned from Hitchcock) is increased by the staccato rhythm of the sequence showing his journey to the airport. The urgent acceleration of the music contributes to the tension as a general shot of a Mercedes pulling away, driven by Pierre's friend Michel, is followed by split-second jump cuts showing it moving at high speed. The journey is punctuated by images of urgency: close-ups of Michel's hands on the wheel; a road sign marked danger; close-up of a gear change, of Michel's hand on the horn as he overtakes, of the windscreen, of the dashboard; then an even sharper sequence of cuts from Michel's hand to his foot on the accelerator and to the windscreen wipers; then Orly airport seen through the windscreen, and finally the race to board the plane, and the sequence ends with a shot of the plane above the clouds as it begins its descent over Lisbon. An extended metaphor, then, not just of the pace and frenzy of modern living in general but illustrating the stresses among which this individual man lives.

Pierre's first glimpse of the 'soft skin' of the air hostess, Nicole, comes after they have exchanged glances in the aircraft: he stares with almost fetishist fascination at her feet, visible under the curtain as she changes her shoes. He then obliges the press photographers at the airport by posing with Nicole, and slots with accustomed ease into his public role of visiting lecturer, television celebrity, inter-

*La Peau Douce*: stress (Jean Desailly as Pierre)

national man of letters and authority on Balzac (an inevitable choice of author for Truffaut). A link between Pierre and Charlie Kohler in *Tirez sur le Pianiste* is provided by the contrast between the suavity and confidence he displays as a public personality and the timidity and uncertainty against which his role-playing can protect him only in impersonal situations – revealed in the sequence showing him and Nicole in the hotel lift. Mounting desire, suppressed, results only in verbal impotence in this most typical Truffaut male. He needs Nicole's unsubtle ploy of dropping her room key to galvanize him into action. Even then he only gazes after her receding figure, and particularly her feet again, as she walks to her room; then he descends in the lift to his own floor and the shoe motif (homage to Buñuel?) is resumed with a rear tracking shot along the corridor of shoes outside the doors, indicating that some rooms are occupied by couples, some by a single person.

In the haven of his own room, with all the lights off, he hesitantly summons the courage to telephone Nicole, stammers an excuse for his impoliteness earlier in the lift, finally (again like Charlie Kohler) blurts out a direct invitation for a drink in the hotel bar – without realizing it is already 1.15 a.m. – and after more politenesses gloomily hangs up. Suddenly his phone rings: Pierre rushes to pick it up, Nicole suggests a rendezvous for the following day – Pierre cannot believe his ears. For the only time in the film he is blissfully happy; as the music swells to a climax, he switches on every possible light and flings himself fully-clothed on to his bed.

The next night Pierre's enthusiasm and confidence as he narrates the life of Balzac to a fascinated Nicole into the early hours of the morning seem to overflow into his relatively positive approach to her seduction, though a second lift sequence almost intimidates him again. Their first tender kiss in Nicole's darkened room, with the two faces in profile and Pierre's finger caressing her features, is Truffaut's familiar designation of a love relationship. Though despite this gentleness, and his usual discreet early fade-out, Truffaut does not entirely dispel the vague sense of disquiet prompted by the sight of a fumbling, diffident, shifty-eyed, middle-aged man about to become the lover of an attractive woman half his age. The seeds of future disaster are already sown in the audience's mind.

Later, it is characteristically left to Nicole to ensure that the relationship continues by giving Pierre her telephone number. The

Pierre and Franca (Nelly Benedetti), symbolically separated . . .

first shot of Pierre's reunion with his wife Franca shows them at the airport, symbolically separated by a glass barrier through which they try to communicate. But on a physical level at least theirs is no arid relationship – Franca's warmth and passion for Pierre contrast with the relative coolness, verging on frigidity, of Nicole. Pierre, though, is now hopelessly immersed in his subconscious need to elevate the trivial-minded Nicole to the planes of perfection found only in fairy-tales: a characteristic he shares with other Truffaut heroes with a preference for fantasy over reality, like Coral in *La Mariée était en noir*, and of course Antoine Doinel, a similar slightly anachronistic dreamer with a taste for nineteenth-century literature. Returning from a clandestine encounter with Nicole at Orly, where his telegram to her declaring his love and the impossibility of living without her (a variation on Antoine's *pneumatique* in *Baisers Volés*) remains unposted, his sheepish apology to Franca for his earlier exasperation results in a passionate embrace which suggests that the marriage is far from dead. Pierre and Nicole, on the other hand, make a very

108

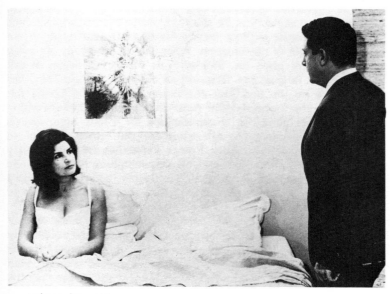

... and growing apart

ill-assorted couple. Their age difference is emphasized by his being content simply to watch her dance, and later by his encounter with a man only slightly older than himself, her father. The furtive nature of their affair is highlighted by their embarrassment when they take a room in a short-stay hotel.

Ironically, their conclusion that what they need is to escape from the pressures of Paris is exactly the solution suggested by Franca to the problem of her own deteriorating relationship with Pierre. The hilariously nightmarish sequence in Rheims, where Pierre is lecturing at the request of Clément, an old friend, is strategically placed at the centre of the film, where it leavens the surrounding atmosphere of hopelessness. Pierre's sense of being trapped and hounded grows moment by moment. He dashes from the official reception to buy stockings for Nicole (always a sign of male enslavement in Truffaut's world), then back to the assembled worthies of the town; survives a bad moment, along with the audience, when he thinks Nicole has come to seek him out in public (Truffaut playing with false clues –

109

again the Hitchcock influence); then is unable to shake off Clément after the lecture and suffers the agony of seeing Nicole propositioned in front of his nose without feeling honest or bold enough to tell Clément the truth of the situation. When the couple finally get away for their country idyll, his 'little girl', as Pierre has begun to call Nicole, feigns fatigue and later, as he clumsily caresses her, lies unresponsive on the bed. Her confession next day of having felt sullied on another occasion after experiencing sexual pleasure with a man, and of her ability to go without sex for a long time, reveals strangely dispassionate characteristics for the 'other woman' to possess; whereas, paradoxically, Franca's appetites are clearly fairly powerful. Pierre's preoccupation with photographing Nicole, on one occasion dashing frantically to sit beside her before the camera clicks, is symptomatic of his need to give a sense of permanence to the affair.

Returning to Paris, the lovers are muted. Pierre's feeling of guilt because his wife knows he has lied to her leads him to be excessively assertive when confronted with Franca's angry desolation. He accepts literally her wild suggestion that they should separate, glad of the opportunity to walk out at once. The slightly larger-than-life situation here; the shocked awareness of having gone too far to withdraw; the stubborn determination to go on playing out roles to the end – all this recurs in Antoine's break-up with his wife in *Domicile Conjugal*.

Pierre is blind to Nicole's increasingly casual treatment of him, and even the visit of her father does not reveal to him that a sort of protective paternalism is at the heart of his own feelings for her (the reverse of the coin of the Antoine-Fabienne relationship in *Baisers Volés*). Meanwhile Franca's attempt to get a temporary reconciliation with Pierre, accepted by him on a physical level but stubbornly resisted as a permanent solution, produces a violent reaction from her which anticipates the ending. Pierre's indirect marriage proposal is not accepted by Nicole, and he is hurt by her offer of a casual relationship instead. Life is closing in on Pierre; a point illustrated obliquely by the incident between Franca and the man who tries to pick her up just after she has seen the photographs of Pierre and Nicole, which is not a gratuitous comic interlude but reveals the dangerous extent of her anger, as well as illustrating the role of chance, again a key feature in this film.

Pierre and Nicole (Françoise Dorléac): obsessive photography and a furtive embrace

As in *Baisers Volés*, we can trace the role of chance in the film as a chain of fortuitous incidents on which the final outcome hinges. Pierre just catches the Lisbon plane which Nicole happens to be on; they happen to be staying at the same hotel and to take the lift together; Pierre casually keeps the book of matches on which he later sees the telephone number which Nicole has written; Franca finds the photographer's ticket when she has Pierre's jacket cleaned; and so on. Chance is of course the basis of much narrative film, but here Truffaut's skill in manipulating it is such that he makes the ending seem inevitable, paradoxically almost *because* chance can now be counted as a factor operating on the fate of the characters. The influence of Hitchcock, apparent in the climate of anxiety generated throughout, is nowhere more powerful than in the final sequence.

The justification for the shooting of Pierre by Franca, with which the film ends, has nothing to do with the fact that it is authenticated by a newspaper account of a similar *crime passionel* which Truffaut had read. It can be seen in terms of dramatic plausibility, as the only solution likely to appeal to the progressively hysterical mind of a spurned, passionate woman. In cinematic terms this final sequence is superbly manoeuvred. Pierre's dithering during the first telephone conversation with his wife's friend Odile about whether to begin again with Franca; the agony for the audience as his second phone call to Franca is delayed; Franca making her preparations with the rifle; the maid slowly and methodically checking that her mistress has left, and the thrill of horror that a murder is inevitably about to be committed. The ritual revenge of Franca produces its cathartic effect on murderer and audience alike.

# 12: Fahrenheit 451

After *La Peau Douce*, it was more than two years before Truffaut shot his next film, an adaptation of Ray Bradbury's science fiction novel *Fahrenheit 451*, which he had wanted to film for some years. The delay was caused mainly by difficulties in setting up the finance (Truffaut had bought the rights in 1962, then sold them to the American producer Lewis Allen, and had expected to make the film in America in 1964). The conditions of the final agreement specified a big budget studio production, to be shot in colour, in the English language and in England. Truffaut had hitherto made only relatively low budget, black and white films in French. His command of English was, and remained, limited, particularly in the context of a film whose centre of interest is its exploration of the problem of language. Yet Truffaut often said that a film is a gamble, not a wager won in advance; and he badly wanted to examine the theme of linguistic and cultural deprivation in a bookless society. So he accepted the challenge and made the film. Ultimately, the problems proved overwhelming.

In Truffaut's adaptation, again in collaboration with Jean-Louis Richard, of Bradbury's novel, it is not the science fiction elements which interest him but the basic situation of a society in which books are banned and the job of firemen is to track them down and burn them. So Bradbury's Mechanical Hound, a machine which can be programmed to hunt and destroy human beings with lethal injections, does not appear in the film. Nor is there any mention of the total annihilation of cities in lightning wars, with the idea of society having to survive a new Dark Age. Truffaut's film, set in the very near future in an unspecified country, is more like an allegory or a moral tale (a feature of the novel, but to a lesser extent). The few futuristic elements, such as the search squad of flying men (a shot so casual that the lines by which they are suspended are clearly visible), the monorail and the television screens which fill a whole wall, are balanced by the late Sixties skirt lengths and even older fire-engines, while the telephones are fashionably antique. By playing down the science fiction emphasis, Truffaut attempted to give the time-lessness of the fairytale to a story which, as the Bradbury novel shows, really needed this extra dimension, afforded by the futur-istic, Brave New World aspects, in order to sustain interest.

Neither the colour nor the big budget studio production gloss is a positive asset. Truffaut said that he shot the film exactly as if it were in black and white, and apart from his fascination with filming flames and the impact of the strident red of the fire-engines, the film gains little from being in colour. True, the softer, more muted tones used for the gentle Book People contrast with the generally harsher colour elsewhere, but there is little sense of the systematic use of colour as a motif or as a demonstration of the theme. The artificiality of some of the studio sets would be credible only if it were reflected throughout the film and could be seen as a feature of the new, hygienic, plastic society. But the interpolation of natural decors, real houses and so on invalidates this possible justification. The use of Julie Christie in the dual roles of Linda, the fireman Montag's wife, and Clarisse, his girl-friend (which seems no more than a publicity gimmick), simply blurs the distinction between the two characters, contrary to the whole spirit of the novel. And the stubborn recalci-trance of Oskar Werner, who refused to accept Truffaut's view of the part of Montag, led (as Truffaut recounts in his published diary kept during the shooting) to the need to edit out a considerable part of his performance. Werner insisted on emphasizing the brutal, fascist elements in the part, whereas Truffaut took these as a point of departure and wanted to stress Montag's vulnerability, and in particular his growing receptivity to language and awakening to literature. One minor example of their quarrel (which reached the point of Truffaut using Werner's double on more than a few occasions) is visible in the apparent discontinuity between successive shots of Montag with hair of normal length and then crop-headed, despite attempts to conceal it by showing him wearing a helmet.

114

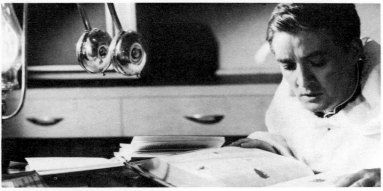

*Fahrenheit 451*: from illiteracy to the rediscovery of language (Oskar Werner)

But the major challenge which Truffaut failed to meet is basic to the success of the whole film: how to prevent the flat, functional characters, whose emotions have been dulled by state suppression of individual expression, from being swamped by a strongly dramatic situation; and how to generate interest in a relationship from which love – because of the paucity of language and hence of communication, arising in turn from the lack of books in particular and state policy in general – is absent. A Truffaut film which is not about love is as typical as a Hitchcock film without suspense. For Truffaut seems to me essentially a director of relationships, and if the film does not work on this level it is difficult for it to work at all.

The one level on which the film does largely work is as a study of the role of language. Truffaut's fascination with the concept of a world without the resonances of language in the form of the printed word, a world inhabited by zombies whose linguistic and thus emotional concepts have atrophied during a new Dark Age, proved difficult to convey in convincing cinematic terms. To succeed entirely, Truffaut would have had to show Montag's faltering development from this primitive state to one of linguistic fluency in a much more prolonged series of images, gradually increasing in rhythm – just as later he showed a much slower progress towards a more limited goal in *L'Enfant Sauvage*. The difference being of course that Montag's starting point is well beyond Victor's point of arrival. In *Fahrenheit 451* Montag is *re*discovering language and books as if for the first time, reawakening in himself a desire for a half-remembered previous state, hinted at in the novel by Clarisse's 'Was it always like this?' Victor in *L'Enfant Sauvage* is starting absolutely from scratch. The transition from semi-literacy to ecstatic fluency in *Fahrenheit 451* is on the whole not sufficiently gradual or awesome. In addition, the information clearly conveyed in the novel – that it is only in living memory that books have come to be banned, so that people do have a residual reading ability – has to be deduced in the film simply from the fact that there are so many books to be burned.

What does come through powerfully is Truffaut's reverence for books, epitomized in Montag's donning of what looks like a monastic habit before settling down to read *David Copperfield*. This reverence for the content of books extends to an obvious affection, which in any other context would verge on fetishism, for books as objects, the touch, the look, the feel, even the smell of them. Under-educated himself and aware that he had 'missed something', Truffaut conveys his pain on seeing a book consumed by flames (anticipated by the Nazi book-burning in *Jules et Jim*) as if it were the incineration of a human being; and at a key moment in the film the two actually occur together. The intensity of this feeling for books eases our acceptance of the process reversed, whereby at the end of the film books are reincarnated as people – a device which out of context might appear naïve.

The film does suffer, however, from being made in the English language by a man who did not speak that language. Every other film by Truffaut is enhanced by his ear for the cadences of language, reflected either in the dialogue or the commentary. Every other film allows him scope for a certain amount of improvisation and flexibility with the spoken word, during the shooting and sometimes even at the post-synchronization stage. Truffaut's normal working method was to write up the next day's script the night before. This was obviously not possible with *Fahrenheit 451*, where he was obliged to adhere rigidly to the prearranged script, and the film is the poorer for it. A film whose theme of linguistic deprivation is already difficult enough to portray is seriously impaired by the linguistic deprivation of its director.

The opening sequence of successive zooms and close-ups of television aerials provides a visual background over which is 'super-imposed' the reading of the credits – a first indication of a media-dominated society where the printed word is banned. The terror inherent in a society in which firemen are judge, jury and executioner is emphasized at once by the pulsating music (by Bernard Herrmann, once Hitchcock's regular composer) as the firemen ruthlessly execute a typical lightning raid, culminating in the ritual public burning of the illegal books. The quasi-fascist aspect of the fire brigade – the crunching jackboots, the unholy zeal, the pleasure in destruction – is noted in passing. But since the central theme is not an anti-censorship protest, nor – despite Werner's attempted interpretation – an anti-Nazi manifesto, Truffaut does not labour the point.

Montag's meeting with his new neighbour Clarisse, in the mono-rail, provides further expository information: Fahrenheit 451 is the temperature at which book paper ignites; and Montag regurgitates

117

Julie Christie in the monorail

all the conformist answers – yes, houses have always been fire-proof; yes, the fireman's job has always been to burn books, which are anti-social rubbish and make people unhappy; no, he is not interested in reading the books he burns, and anyway it is forbidden; of course he is happy. But the impact of this encounter is less powerful than in the novel, where Clarisse, in the individuality of her thinking and her spontaneous, simple happiness, much more clearly disturbs Montag. In the film the contrast between the life-force (Clarisse) and the death-force (Linda) is muted by Truffaut's wish to avoid stereotypes, and also by his instinctive playing down of extremes (which he considered a weakness in *La Sirène du Mississippi*); but this contrast needs to be emphasized here if Clarisse is to be more than a slightly unorthodox pretty girl next door. This lack of contrast may be partly explained by the difficulty for one actress in conveying the emotional range of the two parts; which may also account for the disappearance of the age gap between the two women – in the novel Linda is thirty and Clarisse only sixteen.

Television plays an insidious role in promoting and sustaining a society of mindless hedonists, because of its dominant position as a spurious 'member of the family' in every home. The illusion of intimacy and two-way communication provided by pauses in television plays for gaps in the dialogue to be filled in by twenty thousand Lindas all over the country – who are all then told that they are absolutely marvellous – is as near to real emotions as the nationwide televiewing 'cousins' will ever get. The normal isolation of married couples in bed in Truffaut's films is here pushed to extremes, as Montag reads his strip cartoons while Linda listens to non-stop radio with individual earphones. Linda's overdose of sleeping pills is treated as a routine case by the matey stomach-pump operators. It also allows an opportunity for a kind of clinical rape by machine as her body is stripped by the men to the accompaniment of their bawdy remarks. More voyeuristic satisfaction for the audience is provided by Linda's subsequent frolicsome seduction of Montag, reminiscent of a similar moment (also with Oskar Werner) in *Jules et Jim* and again showing the woman taking the initiative. And the general theme of a society deprived of love is illustrated by shots in the monorail sequence – seen from Montag's viewpoint – of women caressing themselves in solitary compensation.

Montag's clandestine reading of *David Copperfield* marks the

'A society of mindless hedonists': television as a member of the family

beginning of his rebellion. He learns of Clarisse's expulsion from her job as a schoolteacher, because of her unorthodox thinking; then later a scene showing an informant furtively circling round an 'information box' somewhat obviously signposts Linda's denunciation of Montag. His discovery that 'behind each of these books there is a man' leads to the climactic self-immolation scene, where an old woman sets fire to herself amidst her books, dismissed by the enigmatic fire chief because they are fiction, or written by philosophers who are idiots since they never agree, or because they have a socially divisive effect. The role of the fire chief (sinisterly played by Cyril Cusack) is rather ambiguous. There is a good deal of genial sadism in his treatment of Montag, but his own wide knowledge of books suggests possibly over-zealous reading habits in his youth – from the corrupting effects of which he is now pledged to protect society. The passion with which he discusses books, even if he subsequently denounces them, is indicative of the double-think of censorship: dangerous pleasures are accessible only to an incorruptible, self-

Dangerous pleasures: the fire chief finds some books (Cyril Cusack)

styled elite, who are themselves the arbiters of what may corrupt others. Since books are considered potentially subversive, the neat totalitarian solution is to burn them.

Montag's violent reaction to the concealment and frivolous diversions of television, and his reading aloud of *David Copperfield* which moves one of his wife's friends to tears, is seen by the women as further evidence that books make people unhappy. As Clarisse narrowly escapes the forces of repression, Montag's stunned realization that his last mission is to burn books in his own house turns to desperate joy as he destroys the whole house with his flame-gun and the fire chief with it. Television again distorts the gap between fact

121

and fiction, providing vicarious excitement in a mock-up of Montag's death. A substitute is destroyed in front of the cameras, and the nation sees that 'a crime against society has been avenged'.

The escape of the real Montag to join the 'Book People', who live on the outskirts of towns and whose mission is to learn the contents of books by heart, completes the transition from author to book back to living person again, and is held up as a symbol for the survival of the human spirit. But there is a slight sense of over-explicitness in Truffaut's fairytale ending, as 'the first snows of winter' (during the shooting, by a happy accident) fall on a criss-crossing motley of people, some with walkie-talkie radio transmitters, reciting their books aloud in every tongue like a scene from the Tower of Babel. Innocence is suggested, but perhaps too innocently.

At any rate now, at the end of the film, the theoretical possibility of human contact, even love, exists. But Truffaut was not satisfied to leave his study of the relationship between language and emotion at this embryonic stage. And *Fahrenheit 451* can be seen, with hindsight, as an anticipation of the extended thesis of *L'Enfant Sauvage*.

# 13: La Mariée était en noir

From the fairytale land of *Fahrenheit 451*, where love may be dawning, we are transported to another far country, where the ice goddess slaughters five innocents who have slain her love. As this angel of death accomplishes her self-ordained task, we watch fascinated, having suspended not only our disbelief but also our capacity for moral judgment. Our progressive involvement with the success of her multiple murder mission is perhaps Truffaut's major achievement in *La Mariée était en noir*.

The film's basic premise is an unlikely gamble with audience reaction, more audacious even than Hitchcock's killing off of his heroine in the first part of *Psycho*, which causes the audience to switch horses in mid-course. Yet it pays off, and having lost his wager in *Fahrenheit 451* Truffaut wins this one. We do identify almost from the beginning with this inscrutable figure of vengeance, who is not merely unsympathetic in her emotionless efficiency but also morally unjustified in continuing her quest once the relative innocence of her victims has been established. We do accept her on Truffaut's terms − as a woman in whom all springs of humanity abruptly dried on one traumatic occasion, who died as a woman the moment her love died, yet who continues to function with terrifyingly mechanical obduracy in her chosen sphere. The truth emerges that if a film is cleverly enough shot, we will identify with anyone who so dominates the centre of attention.

*La Mariée était en noir* (*The Bride Wore Black*) clearly owes much to Hitchcock (it was made, incidentally, soon after the publication of Truffaut's Hitchcock book). It is adapted from the novel

*The Bride Wore Black* by William Irish (alias Cornell Woolrich) of *Rear Window* fame. The film's music is again by Bernard Herrmann, who wrote distinctive themes for each of the five carefully structured episodes. The audience is manipulated with Hitchcockian ease – the identification phenomenon itself is an impressive achievement – superbly illustrated by our expectation of a happy ending, which Truffaut deliberately contrives and then tantalizingly thwarts. Particularly Hitchcockian is the overall construction, with the resolution being indicated well before the end, as in *Vertigo*, thereby increasing, not diminishing, the suspense of anticipation. But despite the importance of these almost self-consciously Hitchcockian elements, which make the film the most overt of Truffaut's homages to this master, *La Mariée était en noir* differs significantly from most of Hitchcock's films in at least one major respect – the extent to which Truffaut makes the characters speak about anything but the plot. Thus the five victims are not entirely overwhelmed by the sheer mechanics of the construction, but command our sympathy as human beings. Truffaut explained this humanity as part of his debt to Renoir, and modestly described the film as another attempt to synthesize the best aspects of his two mentors. But under scrutiny, and in its development from Irish's fairly run-of-the-mill thriller, the originality of Truffaut's treatment emerges as much more than the total of the Hitchcock plus Renoir equation.

The transposition of the novel from America to a never-never land occasionally recognizable as France poses no problems. The main structural difference is in the film's rejection of the ponderous police enquiry section which Irish inserts at the end of each chapter. Truffaut does not bring in the police until after the third murder, and then not in a major role. The avenging woman, Julie Kohler in the film, appears and disappears at will, as befits a fairytale heroine. The progressive revelation, by flashbacks, of the motive for the murders is the key to the film's carefully controlled suspense. Some of the novel's irrelevant minor characters have been pared away; and Irish's fifth victim, a novelist, is replaced in the film by a car dealer, perhaps because of Truffaut's view (expressed in connection with *Domicile Conjugal* though disregarded in *L'Homme qui Aimait les Femmes* and *L'Amour en Fuite*) that writers' lives are not the stuff of which films are made. The novel's highly tortuous final revelation dots the i's and crosses the t's in conventional thriller style; Truffaut

*La Mariée était en noir*: innocents to the slaughter

avoids this by revealing the motivation of the heroine in mid-film, and thus paradoxically, as in *Tirez sur le Pianiste*, maintains the suspense to the end.

The opening stills of Julie Kohler, naked and expressionless in artistic pose, flick by with machine-like precision, establishing her at the outset as a vision of womankind, statuesque and unattainable. The Wedding March is played on an organ; Julie attempts suicide; then, dressed all in black (and with a Hitchcockian emphasis on the angles of her suitcase, shots of her gloves, close-ups of her legs and so on) she simulates departure from the unknown town, and the way is clear for the action proper.

As the film proceeds, it resembles increasingly one woman's personal vendetta on behalf of all women against the masculine sex. In a reversal of the situation in *Les Mistons*, Julie hunts down five men, each representing different aspects of masculine behaviour towards women. The links between the five seem tenuous; but they all happened to be involved in the accidental shooting of David, Julie's

125

husband of five minutes, as the wedding party stood on the church steps. Julie's revenge mission is accomplished with an intransigence and an absolutism reminiscent of Jeanne Moreau's other major Truffaut role as Catherine in *Jules et Jim*. Like Catherine, she takes the initiative in manipulating vulnerable males. The difference between them is Julie's virginity, whereas Catherine lived according to her own code of sexual liberty. But both go 'to the end of themselves' and scorn the consequences. And both bring about the destruction of the men by whom they are surrounded.

Audience reaction to the death of Julie's first victim, inappropriately named Bliss, tends to be one of intrigued curiosity and mild surprise rather than of horror. Well, she killed him, after luring him on to a balcony by appealing to his gullibility and easily flattered vanity. Perhaps it will serve as a moral lesson to all such men-about-town who cannot withhold their services from an attractive and apparently inaccessible woman even during their own engagement celebrations. Perhaps Bliss' fiancée (Gilberte, like Jim's fiancée in *Jules et Jim*) has lost just another fickle male, whose casual collection of women is exceeded only by that of his friend, Corey. Their happy exchange of one of Truffaut's favourite aphorisms, 'When you've seen one, you've seen them all,' followed by Bliss' tape-recording of his fiancée crossing her legs in nylon stockings (another Truffaut fetish), marks them out as men for whom women are sexual objects. The humiliation of Corey by Julie, as she pours into a potted plant the glass of water he has brought her and then asks for another, is a small delight of revenge; and her pushing Bliss to his death, with the enigmatic phrase 'I am Julie Kohler' ringing in his ears, seems in the context little more than one woman's blow for liberation. We are interested but neutral.

Linked to her capacity for elusiveness is Julie's ability to transform herself by clothing, make-up and hair style into the type of woman most likely to appeal to each man in turn. So she establishes that Coral, her second victim, is a romantic who takes refuge from mediocre reality in dreams, which is the only world in which the ideal woman, for whom he is looking, exists. She engineers her meeting with him in a private box at a concert, where he is totally overwhelmed by her fairytale princess appearance, just like Antoine Doinel, smitten in a similar musical setting. Coral is presented throughout in a sympathetic light. He is a middle-aged bachelor,

'The type of woman most likely to appeal . . .': Julie (Jeanne Moreau) adapts to her victims (Claude Rich, Jean-Claude Brialy; Michel Bouquet; Charles Denner)

living alone in a cramped apartment; he pencils in the level of gin in his bottle daily, and does not notice that the maid waters it down; he looks into two mirrors as he carefully combs his hair back over his bald patch; he adores this vision of woman, calling her 'magical' and 'beautiful, too beautiful for me', as she dances in front of him, like Nicole for another middle-aged man in *La Peau Douce*. He is poignantly, pathetically in love, perhaps for the first and certainly the last time in his life. Our uneasiness that Julie should have awakened him to love, only to poison him coldly and watch him die in agony with a gratuitous sadism which transcends even her avenging *femme fatale* role, estranges us from her cause at this point; the more so after the further revelation of Coral's chance implication in the shooting, as the camera pans in flashback down the church steeple and the bridegroom clutches at his chest.

With the third victim, Morane, the pendulum begins to swing slightly the other way again, partly because of Julie's telephone call to the police to secure the release of the innocent schoolteacher suspect, partly because Truffaut develops the part of Morane to emphasize his least sympathetic aspects. Michel Lonsdale's interpretation splendidly anticipates his performance as Monsieur Tabard in *Baisers Volés*: a stolid, affluent, self-made politician who, like Antoine's father in *Les Quatre Cents Coups*, tries to instil into his child that there are winners and losers in life's rat race and the race begins at school. So he seeks to extract from Julie, in her guise as his son's teacher, her criteria for awarding stars for progress. Like Monsieur Darbon in *Antoine et Colette*, he needs to reassure himself that his own lack of stars at school has not hindered him in life. His hypocrisy and lechery are brilliantly conveyed in the short sequence which begins with his injunction to his son not to forget to say his prayers as he is put to bed. Then, as a violent storm erupts outside, he slyly decides that since his wife will now have reached her mother's and since, as he blindly imagines, women 'usually go for politicians', he will perhaps 'forget France for an hour . . .'

Julie's explanation of her motives, recalled by a sudden peal of thunder like the fatal rifle shot, is accompanied by the most detailed flashback so far, showing through the telescopic rifle sights exactly how the accident on the church steps happened. Her key phrase – 'For you it's an old story, for me it recurs every night' – prefaces her monologue about her pure, childhood love for David, shown with

'The thrill of anticipation': Julie in prison

slow-motion shots of them in white playing together as children. This account of the shattering of innocence occurs while Morane is slowly choking to death in the cupboard in which she has sealed him – during an innocent children's game. It recalls Plyne's monologue on the sullying of pure love in *Tirez sur le Pianiste*, delivered while he is squeezing Charlie's head in a stranglehold. But this doing to death of victims who are now seen to be innocent, or at most only marginally guilty, is not sufficient to purge Julie of her pain. The audience sympathizes with her now in the intensity of her suffering, likes her for her humanity in not allowing the teacher to suffer in her place, and fears for her safety as the arrival of Corey, just as she is departing from the airport, renders her for the first time vulnerable, a fugitive and potential victim herself. Pausing only to strengthen her faltering resolve at the confessional, and feeling now 'neither fear nor remorse', Julie resumes her mission, but is thwarted in her attempt to kill the car-dealer, Delvaux, by his untimely arrest and imprisonment.

In the fifth encounter, with the artist Fergus, Truffaut really gives

129

his taste for audience manipulation full rein. The symbolism of Julie's posing for him as Diane the Huntress needs no emphasis. This connoisseur of women is nevertheless predictably ensnared by the chaste, inviolate goddess. Minor tremors of apprehension inspired by the reappearance of Corey, who is 'sure he's seen Julie somewhere before', are quelled by the laughter which greets this stock phrase and also his next bit of patter about all women being whores 'except my mother, who is a saint', and then, 'When you've seen one . . .' But all hope of a 'happy' ending, threatened by two false climaxes as Julie's arrow quivers on her bow, is finally thwarted. Corey's sudden recall of memory, triggered off when he pours a drink into a potted plant, is too late to save Fergus from martyrdom, his heart pierced by an arrow.

Our reproach of Truffaut for having thus apparently misled us is soon replaced by our identification with Julie in the final accomplishment of her task. The thrill of anticipation, as we follow the progress of the food trolley from the female to the male block in the prison where she has deliberately allowed herself to be taken, is a masterfully prolonged moment of suspense. We have approved of her appropriating the huge vegetable knife; we now await nervously the victim's scream in the moment of silence which precedes the sudden eruption of the Wedding March, played on the organ, as Truffaut holds the final shot of the prison corridor. Our final identification with Julie is complete.

# 14: La Sirène du Mississippi

Inside any Irish tale there may lurk a bigger one. Take for example the episode with the pathetic bachelor, Coral, in *The Bride Wore Black*, blow it up, and you have something like Irish's *Waltz into Darkness*, or *La Sirène du Mississippi* in the French translation on which Truffaut's film is based. The significance of the Mississippi half of the title is lost in Truffaut's version, where the action is transferred from the American Deep South to the French island of Réunion and mainland France. Rather unsatisfactorily, Truffaut simply gives the name 'La Sirène du Mississippi' to the boat which brings Louis' bride-to-be to the island, thereby seeming to attribute to it an importance which it does not in fact have in the film. The title is presumably retained because 'Sirène' is an appropriate word to describe yet another wrecker of men.

If Louis in the film is unconvincingly snatched from his last waltz into the ultimate darkness, the fate which awaits him in the novel, it is because of Truffaut's views on what constitutes an acceptable cinematic ending. 'You must never end a spectacle on a downward curve. Life may descend into degradation, old age and death, but a spectacle must exalt and uplift.' Hence the preponderance of guardedly 'open endings' in Truffaut, with *La Peau Douce* as the only example of finality. Even *Tirez sur le Pianiste* and *Jules et Jim* imply at least the possibility that the upward curve might be about to begin.

The film faithfully respects the construction and proportions of the novel. The events portrayed are almost identical with those in the novel, as are the appearances, disappearances and reappearances of the main characters. But rather than attempt a literal adaptation of a very long novel, Truffaut reproduces its essence by filming representative scenes. In the process, the extreme contrast between the ruthless female and the weak, naïve male is modified. Truffaut accepts Irish's conventional Hollywood thriller framework, but within it he is free to speak once again about love, as he does in all his films. Louis and Marion, though involved in an abnormal situation, are a modern couple whose fluctuating relationship is not intrinsically different in kind, though quite different in degree, from that of the Doinels in *Domicile Conjugal*. Truffaut called his film the story of 'a degradation, by love', but it is a pale reflection of the long line of cinematic antecedents which he intended to emulate, from Sternberg's *Blue Angel* via Renoir's *La Chienne* to Godard's *A Bout de Souffle* and *Pierrot le Fou* (Jean-Paul Belmondo appears in both these Godard films and in Truffaut's film, and his downfall is brought about by Marianne in *Pierrot le Fou* and by Marion here). Within the strong dramatic situation Truffaut has scope to explore the intimacies of the couple relationship, in which for the first time there is no distracting 'other' man or woman. He can concentrate on the closeness and distances of their communication, their long silences, their frustrations and disillusionments and crises, all the shared experience which finally makes them indispensable to each other. He is free to write the dialogue for each scene the night before, as he prefers, and is helped by being able to shoot the film in chronological order. Above all, behind the flimsy mask, his self-revelation through the character of Louis is again as complete as in the Antoine Doinel cycle.

The opening credits sequence has echoes – visual, verbal and thematic – of a number of Truffaut's earlier films. The confusion of voices reading advertisements from the personal column of a newspaper recalls the babel at the end of *Fahrenheit 451*. The rapidly accelerating rhythm and intimacy of the correspondence between Louis and Julie Roussel develops the love by correspondence anecdote in *Jules et Jim*. The idea of any love being acceptable provided it relieves the solitude of this thirty-seven-year-old bachelor (the same age as Truffaut at the time of shooting) recalls the desperation of Coral in *La Mariée était en noir*. While the later revelation of the death of Louis' first love years before (on the eve of their wedding in the novel – seemingly an obsession with Irish) reflects the situation in *Tirez sur le Pianiste*.

*La Sirène du Mississippi*: the intimacies of the couple relationship (Jean-Paul Belmondo, Catherine Deneuve)

Truffaut claims that he dedicated the film to Renoir because whenever he was faced with a difficulty of improvisation he asked himself how Renoir would have solved it. There are also numerous references to Renoir throughout the film. A clip from *La Marseillaise* illustrates the moment in history (the 'Réunion') from which the island is said to get its name; though all this seems a pretty tenuous justification for some of the travelogue shots of the island, as if Truffaut had become aware for the first time of the potential of colour photography. (Yves Saint Laurent as costume adviser is another glossy, super-production irrelevancy which the film and Truffaut could well have done without.) Touches of truculent humour, typical of Renoir, such as the sequence in which Catherine Deneuve strips to the waist in an open sports car and a passing motorist drives into a post, are characteristic of Truffaut's frequently jocular asides on a theme − here women as the cause of men's downfall. One is reminded of the comic gangster's revenge quest against all women for the same reason in *Tirez sur le Pianiste*; and a similar scene features in the script of *La Peau Douce*, though it was not used in the final version. There is also a direct reference to Renoir's *Le Crime de Monsieur Lange* in the title of the film, *Arizona Jim*, which Louis goes to see in Aix. Again, the open ending purports to be a homage to the last shot of *La Grande Illusion*. And finally there is an obvious thematic link with *La Chienne*.

The scope of this chapter does not allow further exploration of all the other allusions and resonances which make of any Truffaut film a journey through its director's conscious and unconscious cinematic memory. The other two itineraries which this film traces are the geographical one, from Réunion to the Swiss frontier via Nice, Antibes, Aix and Lyon; and the psychological one, the progress of a passion which transcends the various stages of degradation through which it is purged, to emerge finally in a state of purity.

Everything which happens in the film is seen as usual from Louis' viewpoint, and his anxiety throughout is thus shared by the audience. From the moment when he initially fails to recognize 'Julie Roussel' among the passengers on the boat; through his acceptance of her explanation for her first 'adorable lie'; the ring which sticks on her finger during the marriage ceremony; their prolonged retention of the 'vous' form of address; his calling her paternally his 'little Julie' (cf. *La Peau Douce*); her preference for coffee, which she had

134

claimed to dislike; her postponing the opening of her trunk and later writing to her sister – through all this we feel as much disquiet as Louis, and often, in good Hitchcockian style, Truffaut allows us to be one step ahead. Her indifference to the death of the canary which she had brought with her is not forgotten as we watch her 'innocently' seduce her husband, who finds her – again – 'adorable'. Later, after her unexplained beating up by a man unknown to us and Louis' insistence that his bank account be a joint one with her, he still finds her 'adorable', spells out that it means 'worthy of adoration', and, despite finding that she still has not written to her sister, tells her on the telephone that he loves her – ironically when he is on the edge of disaster. The conversation ends with a 'Me too' – 'Tenderly' – 'Me too' exchange of the kind which signifies a real love idyll in Truffaut's films (a similar conversation was removed from the final version of *La Peau Douce*, and one appears near the end of *Domicile Conjugal*).

Louis' belated realization that his bird has flown, with all his money, leads him to a ritualistic burning of her white underwear (later she is seen in a black dress) and a bitter revenge quest, spurred on by the arrival of Berthe, sister of the real Julie Roussel. To help him, Louis engages a private detective called Comolli (also the name of *Cahiers'* editor-in-chief), which allows Truffaut an opportunity to use some of the material left over from his researches into private detectives made for *Baisers Volés*; and also, in Comolli's fanatical determination to pursue his mission to the end, recalls the dedication of Julie Kohler in *La Mariée était en noir*. The central reconciliation scene – which begins with Louis finding himself unable to press the trigger to kill his wife, and ends, after he has heard her life story and learned that the real Julie Roussel was not ignorant of his wealth, with his discovery that his wife has fallen in love with him – recalls the opening anecdote in *Tirez sur le Pianiste*, where the man fell in love with his wife two years after their marriage.

A period of renewed intimacy, punctuated by a marital frolic and the use of the 'tu' mode of address, is a brief second honeymoon. 'It lasts so short a time. It happens only once and then goes away never to return,' says Irish. Truffaut expresses it by commenting on the hopeful idealists who try to establish 'definitive happiness' for themselves in seven lines of a newspaper advertisement, while Louis recognizes that his wife, whose real name turns out to be Marion, has brought him the 'provisional' (as in *Baisers Volés*) and that life is not

135

Fanatical determination: detective on the trail (Michel Bouquet); Julie and money; and (*opposite*) Louis poisoned

so simple. It is chance, not choice; but the fireside scene of tender love in which Louis reverently touches Marion's features, again in profile, reveals that he has revised his preconceptions of love and is, as he says, 'enchanted in the full sense of the word' to know her. His subsequent shooting of Comolli is 'proof' to Marion that he has 'gone to the end of himself', and she at last wants him sexually (echoes of *Bonnie and Clyde* – Irish incidentally calls his heroine Bonnie – in the association between the revolver and masculine potency. One thinks also of Charlie's brothers in *Tirez sur le Pianiste*, who welcome him as 'one of them' because he has killed a man). But Louis still has vestiges of his previous social attitudes, which prevent him from appreciating Marion's scorn for 'men who work' and her hatred of the mediocrity of poverty.

The renewed intimacy lasts only as long as the money which Louis has brought from the sale of his shares in the factory to his partner. He is finally reduced to asserting his rights as Marion's husband by refusing to let her go from the chalet in the Alps (also the gangsters'

137

hideout at the end of *Tirez sur le Pianiste*) where they have taken refuge from the police. He reads Balzac's *La Peau de Chagrin*, with its warnings of 'excessive desires, intemperances, joys which kill, griefs which cause you to live too much; for evil is perhaps only a violent pleasure'; and then, from a comic strip *Snow White and the Seven Dwarfs*, he realizes that his wife is poisoning him for his insurance policy. Yet this perception prompts him to seek to forgive her, accept his fate, and ask her to finish him off – a parallel to her response to him when he first tracked her down after her disappearance from Réunion. And his assertion of his love for her, as she is and despite everything, awakens in her for the first time in her life the awareness that she loves him too.

Irish's couple find each other too late to save Louis' life. But Truffaut's couple exit hand-in-hand through the snow, heading for the Swiss frontier, growing dimmer and dimmer against the snow, and fading at last into silhouettes. This walk into the equivalent of an eternal sunset, however much it may strain our credulity, at least offers the possibility for continuing a love which Irish, with greater realism perhaps, found too strong and pure for this world.

# 15: L'Enfant Sauvage

Many of Truffaut's heroes start from a position inside society and move to a point somewhere on the outer edges – because society rejects them (as in the case of Antoine in *Les Quatre Cents Coups*), or because they in turn are driven by the force of events to reject society (Montag in *Fahrenheit 451*, Louis and Marion in *La Sirène du Mississippi*). In *L'Enfant Sauvage* the direction is reversed. Efforts are made to assimilate a dumb, partially deaf 'savage' into society. He must be broken in from his wild state, taught a verbal language and trained in social behaviour. For his own good, and also as a scientific experiment, the wild child is to be 'civilized', according to nineteenth-century notions of the process. Expressed here in one film are many of Truffaut's most fundamental preoccupations – the link between language and emotion; innocence versus learning; the individual versus society – with a possible key provided by the autobiographical thread.

*Fahrenheit 451* was Truffaut's expression of the need for communication and the fragility of the means available. People are lost when they cannot talk to each other. Montag and Linda had only a debased, dead language; but their relationship is rich in comparison with the possibilities of human contact for the wild child, Victor, who even at the end of the film still has virtually no verbal language and can communicate his needs and affections only on a rudimentary level. His inner solitude is intact. As Léna says of Charlie in *Tirez sur le Pianiste*, 'Even when he's with someone, he is alone.'

Was the experiment worthwhile? Doctor Itard, who conducts it in the spirit of eighteenth-century rational enlightenment, appears

*L'Enfant Sauvage*: the wild child at bay (Jean-Pierre Cargol)

to think that it was. Despite temporary doubts about the 'sterile curiosity of men which snatched [Victor] from his innocent and happy life', he continues with the exercises and at the end of the film says he will go on doing so. More surprisingly, Truffaut appears to endorse Itard's view.

It is a matter of opinion whether Victor in his wild state was happy, the noble savage, or merely pitiful. The debate raises philosophical and sociological questions (about what is specifically, intrinsically 'human' in human nature; about how far supposedly 'human' emotions can be attributed to a near-animal; about whether there is a link between this idea and the 'pathetic fallacy' concept) which are beyond the scope of this book. The evidence in the opening sequence is inconclusive, though it does show a being apparently in tune with his natural habitat. What is certain is that his forcible removal from this environment leads him to experience feelings of nostalgia, rebellion and frustration for the first time. At the end of the film he is in limbo, neither savage nor man. Even if the experiment had been

140

The learning process

totally successful in curing Victor's dumbness and giving him a chance of some human contact, its basic premise could still be questioned. As it is, in the light of what Truffaut called the experiment's 'partial success' (valid in scientific terms – but is Victor really better off?), it is difficult to share his optimism.

The key to Truffaut's attitude may lie in the fact that he was carried away by a sense of excitement about the learning process itself and did not fully examine the aim of the exercise. This may be partially explained again in terms of the strong autobiographical thread in the film. The important thing is not to be deceived by the decoy in the shape of Truffaut himself, appearing for the first time as an actor in his own film, into thinking that Truffaut the actor here equals Truffaut the man. For the key to the interpretation of Truffaut's self-revelation in this film arguably lies in the formula: Wild Child equals Truffaut (the man); Dr Itard (played by Truffaut the actor) equals André Bazin. According to this interpretation, the fascination of the film for Truffaut lies in the process of creation, or

141

Testing a sense of justice: Victor punished by his mentor (François Truffaut)

re-creation, itself, whereby a human being (himself) is freed from his shackles and becomes a new being. Without straining the parallel by a too literal comparison of all the details, Bazin, by moulding, instructing, guiding and judging Truffaut as a young man, fulfilled the Itard, surrogate father role in Truffaut's life. The unhappiness which was certainly an intrinsic part of Truffaut's own education – to which he often referred in interviews – here seems to be minimized by him and interpreted as a necessary part of the educative process. Perhaps for this reason Victor's original state is left ambiguous, and Truffaut is blind to the pessimism behind the apparently 'open' ending. *L'Enfant Sauvage*, like *Les Quatre Cents Coups*, seems above all autobiographical and only incidentally or even unintentionally a work of social criticism.

The opening dedication to Jean-Pierre Léaud is the first clue to the implications of the film. The subsequent caption, proclaiming the story's authenticity, refers to the fact that the film closely follows the *Mémoire et Rapport sur Victor de l'Aveyron*, written in 1801 and

1806 by Dr Jean Itard; though clearly on another level its claim to authenticity is that it is one of the most detailed self-portraits that Truffaut produced. The prologue provides the necessary expository information before Truffaut can come to grips with the scenes of confrontation and the series of exercises which are the essence of the film.

The slow opening of the iris in the initial shot, showing a peasant woman gathering mushrooms in a forest, gradually reveals more of her surroundings. Our fear that she is not alone grows as cracklings and rustlings are heard on the soundtrack. The camera pans and tracks through sunlight and shadow made sinister by our apprehensions, like an animal scenting its prey. A louder cracking sound; a vague animal shape scratching at the earth and emitting curious grunts; panic and flight of the peasant; a long tracking shot to the object of her terror — a naked boy about twelve, his body covered in scars, very long black hair, face and body caked with dirt, quivering nostrils. He moves on all fours and stuffs his mouth with the abandoned mushrooms, lies full-length to drink from a stream, very quickly climbs a tree, the impression of animal-like speed being reinforced by the swift pan of the camera which follows him; cut to a shot of sunlight glistening through leafy treetops, then a close-up of the 'savage's' face seen through the leaves as he observes all that is going on, then scratches his back against the trunk. A very slow backward-tracking shot frames him as the sun gradually disappears, the final closing of the iris and total blacking out of the screen coinciding with the end of the camera movement.

This opening appeals to twentieth-century nostalgia for a mythical age of innocence, as depicted in Rousseau's 'happy savage', uncorrupted by society and thereby posing a threat to the values of that society by his very existence. (The sense of nostalgia is of course increased by Truffaut's use of the iris.) In particular, the association between happiness and nature, as in Renoir, is one of Truffaut's favourite themes, and there is a strong resemblance between the mobile woodland shots of sun glinting through foliage in this film and some of the most lyrical moments in *Jules et Jim*.

Initial audience sympathy for the child, which will be maintained throughout, is enhanced by the scenes of his capture by the peasants, whose boots and gaiters are often shown in menacing close-up. In contrast with the harsh animal world, and also that of the hostile and 'uncivilized' peasants, is the first shot of Dr Itard in his study, reading aloud about the child's capture and standing by an anatomical diagram of the human skull. His desire to examine the child in Paris, in order to determine 'the degree of intelligence and the nature of the ideas of an adolescent, deprived from childhood of all education because of having lived entirely separated from individuals of his own kind', is the first revelation of the essentially scientific nature of Itard's enquiry. The audience is kept informed of the reasons for each experiment by the use of readings (off) by Truffaut, in a fast, neutral monotone, from a newspaper or more often from Itard's diary; the special prose style of Itard's original reports is thus preserved, and also the essentially literary flavour of the linking passages which punctuate the film, as in *Jules et Jim* and later in *Les Deux Anglaises et le Continent*. The deliberate restraint in most of the shots of the doctor reflects the film's quasi-documentary style – appropriate to a scientific experiment; in contrast, the rare dramatic moments seem to be intensified. For once Truffaut seems scarcely conscious of audience reaction, immersed in his need to make the film for himself; so that in its austere classicism, with the camera often static and simply recording what happens in front of it, *L'Enfant Sauvage* is to some extent reminiscent of Straub's 'minimal' cinema.

Truffaut's easy condemnation of the more apparent excesses of eighteenth century society (such as the prison in which the child is tied up by his ankle, the jeering peasants who beat him, and the comic insert showing 'le tout Paris' flocking to see the spectacle of the child and inane comments in official reports about the likelihood of the savage's amazement at 'the beauties of the capital', together with the opinion that the child is insane) paves the way for his apparent acceptance of the assumptions about education on which Itard bases his approach. The child's transfer from prison to the Institute of Deaf Mutes in Paris, where he is catalogued like an object by Itard's colleague Pinel (and all this within the general prison of society), parallels Antoine Doinel's progress and institutional documentation in *Les Quatre Cents Coups*. The savage's indifference to loud noises but response to the cracking of a nut is recorded, and Itard theorizes that his dumbness is not inherent but induced by his isolation from society. The experiment with the mirror and the apple, in which the child finally understands and snatches the real fruit,

144

seems to Itard to reveal something of his educability; and this slight progress is significantly accompanied by a gentle woodwind theme.

The guided visit to this celebrated child, lorded over by the male nurse and punctuated by the child's biting of one of the visitors, is one of Truffaut's few concessions to the audience in what is otherwise a bleak if always fascinating film. Other scenes establish that the child will not eat from a bowl or sleep in a bed, but seems happy playing in the garden in a torrential storm and drinking in the rain. Itard succeeds in gaining responsibility for the child, and with the aid of his housekeeper, Madame Guérin, tries to educate him in his house outside Paris. The remainder of the film is contained within the semi-documentary format of commentary, experiment, reaction, noting of progress made – all directed by Itard with apparent omniscience. He rarely questions the morality of what he is doing, but assumes as a point of departure that the 'education' he is inculcating into the child is of itself good, and therefore that the suffering and anguish which the child undergoes in this crash civilization course is justified because it is for his own good. Itard is a man of his times, whose application of the principles of scientific rationalism to this human specimen is imbued with a spirit of fervent curiosity which often seems stronger than his humanism. He may rationalize his apparent near-cruelty as kindness in disguise, but it is left to Mme Guérin and her simple maternal affection to provide the child with the real milk of human kindness. Meanwhile Itard is captivated, and exalted by every sign of the child's 'progress'.

Everything the child does is for the first time; the process is like witnessing the re-enactment of key episodes in the history of the human race. First, physical actions: unimportant, even trivial in isolation, but in this context cumulatively affecting. His hair, toenails and fingernails are cut, his shoulders are gradually straightened; he never weeps (which Itard interprets as a sign of the absence of any 'moral affection'), and he is insensitive to heat; he learns to walk upright, to drink soup from a bowl, but has his first fit of frustrated rebellion (one of the few scenes reminiscent of Penn's *The Miracle Worker*, despite their obvious similarity of theme) when he is made to wear shoes. As the softening-up process continues, he needs to wear clothes in order to keep warm. Itard's reward and punishment methods continue. The child's joy in being liberated for his daily walks in the country to see Itard's neighbour Lémeri is emotively evoked by the Vivaldi theme music, which highlights Itard's pleasure at the joyful moments of progress almost as if this chamber music for mandolin and flute were a gloss illustrating the pleasures of civilization. The child's 'progress' continues, with a few relapses. He learns how to ask for milk, plays games requiring memory and concentration; and his apparent response to the sound 'o' brings one of the first overt acknowledgments that he is a human being when he is given the name Victor. The elaboration of a language, patiently and systematically but by pedagogic methods which might have been questionable even at the end of the eighteenth century, is certainly frustrating in a twentieth century educational context. There are signs that Victor's deafness is only partial, and one ecstatic moment reveals him banging a drum and ringing a bell in time with Itard. The exhausting rhythm of the exercises continues, unremittingly, though on one occasion Victor is so bored that he leaves the room and climbs a tree before his teacher notices his absence. The huge step from a drawing of an object to its alphabetic representation reduces Victor to another frenzy of frustration and, not surprisingly, when confronted with a set of letters carved in wood, to a fit of nervous rage verging on epilepsy. A later shot of him, face upturned again in the pouring rain, wild with joy, on which the iris closes, recalls the superficiality of the civilizing process and the strength of Victor's nostalgia for his former state. Yet he then shows tenderness to his master, taking Itard's hand and raising it to his eyes, forehead and then the whole of his face, in Truffaut's usual gesture signifying love. Itard next day locks him in a cupboard, and notes in his diary that Victor wept, for the first time. As Victor weeps, Itard's rage and regret for the 'sterile curiosity of men' is one of his rare moments of self-doubt. Victor finds solace in a return to the garden, face upturned as if worshipping the moon, then swaying round and gambolling on all fours.

The calm voice of Itard reacting to Victor's invention of a chalk holder ('Victor has just invented something. Victor is an inventor') seems to burst out triumphantly in this restrained setting, as if heralding a major accomplishment of the race. Then Victor's increasing skill in the fetching-of-objects game is accompanied by an acceleration in the music and the cutting, so that the whole sequence ends in another burst of triumph (the technique here recalls the 'coup

'Nostalgia for his former state': Victor baying at the moon

de foudre' sequence in *Antoine et Colette*). After this joyful moment, Itard's test of Victor's sense of justice – he punishes him unjustly, shuts him in the cupboard, and then rejoices when Victor bites him on his release, thus proving his elevation from the 'savage' to the 'moral' state – seems to be pushing the spirit of the scientific method to the limit.

Victor's final attempt to escape to freedom recalls that of Antoine at the end of *Les Quatre Cents Coups* in its poignancy and melancholy, and particularly in its revelation of Victor's solitude in an aerial shot of him running across a field of stubble towards the forest, from civilization to the wilds. But he has now grown unused to life in his old habitat, and so returns to Itard, who welcomes him with the acknowledgment that Victor is now in the intermediate state between the savage and the man, just as Antoine was suspended between adolescence and manhood. His calm final assertion – 'Tomorrow we will continue the exercises' – implies that the experiment was worth attempting; just as it was also worthwhile for

147

Truffaut to delve again into his own childhood. But this ending, as we have seen, is rather more 'open' than Truffaut realized.

The real Victor lived to the age of forty in Paris, and was able to perform simple, menial tasks. François Truffaut lived to the age of fifty-two in Paris and continued to make films. In 1970, the same year as *L'Enfant Sauvage*, he made *Domicile Conjugal*. He then tried to take a long rest from films, which lasted only until the spring of 1971, by which time he had realized that quite simply he was unhappy when he was not making films. In addition, a project which he had been nurturing for a number of years now seemed ripe for fruition.

# 16: Les Deux Anglaises et le Continent

If *L'Enfant Sauvage* is the summation of Truffaut's preoccupation with language, communication and the individual in society, then *Les Deux Anglaises et le Continent*, which he made in 1971, is another summit for him in the sphere of the literary and psychological love film.

A comparison with *Jules et Jim* makes itself immediately. The films are based on the only two novels written by Henri-Pierre Roché – *Jules et Jim* in 1953 and *Les Deux Anglaises et le Continent* in 1956 (his other work, *Don Juan*, was published under the pseudonym Jean Roc in 1921). The two novels are largely autobiographical, drawing on Roché's own diaries and notebooks. It is known, for instance, that the character of Jim in *Jules et Jim* was based largely on the author; and Roché uses a footnote in his second novel, at the point where the hero, Claude Roc, says he will write a book about his experiences one day, to explain that this was done fifty-three years later – in the present book. Truffaut uses this same footnote as a pretext for showing in the film the publication of Claude Roc's *Jérôme et Julien*, obviously a thinly disguised *Jules et Jim*.

Truffaut's film (called *Anne and Muriel* in English) is based not only on the novel but also on Roché's unpublished private diaries, to which he had access. For Roché the two novels were evidently fused in his mind, and the overlap between them is considerable. Truffaut's two films are similarly interpenetrated, and any discussion of *Les Deux Anglaises et le Continent* must take account of its many echoes of *Jules et Jim*.

Truffaut had to prune from the novel much more than in the

case of *Jules et Jim*, in order again to concentrate attention on the central triangular relationship. There is no attempt, for instance, to evoke turn-of-the-century London, which figures prominently in the novel. The film was shot on location in Paris and Normandy, which supplies the wild beauty of the 'Welsh' countryside. On the few occasions when Truffaut has English people talking English, their conversations are slightly stilted; as was clear in *Fahrenheit 451*, Truffaut's ear for the spoken language fails him amid the unfamiliar Anglo-Saxon cadences, and he wisely reduces these English conversation scenes to a minimum. The relationship between the Frenchman ('the Continent') and the two English sisters, Anne and Muriel Brown, is more fully developed in the novel, as one would expect, and the same is true of the strong initial attraction between Claude and Anne. Again, some parts of the novel, such as the idea of being *un curieux* by profession and the tumultuous life-story of the non-stop Thérèse, have already been used in *Jules et Jim* and so are omitted here. Other incidents, such as Claude's first sexual experience — with Pilar in Madrid — are cut, perhaps because Truffaut might have thought them too explicit. The omission of Pilar is actually a positive asset — Muriel's reasons for refusing Claude initially are thus less specific — and the film gains in subtlety what it loses in explicitness. The obstacles which keep the characters apart in the film are rarely physical; more often it is their mental blocks and uncertainty about their feelings which prevent them from coming together. In this respect the film's atmosphere is very reminiscent of Gide's *La Porte Etroite* (one man loved by two sisters; self-sacrifice, self-deception and repressed sexuality all round; the frustration of any sexual consummation in the Gide and its postponement until too late in the Truffaut).

Details spelled out in the novel, like the Oedipal possessiveness of Claude's mother, are economically hinted at in the film; and all the novel's minor characters are pruned. On the other hand, Truffaut preserved the flavour of the novel by retaining almost all the language, whether dialogue or reported speech, though it is often attributed to different characters or contexts. One occasion when the film might profitably have followed the novel occurs during the trial separation between Claude and Muriel. Roché effectively divides the page into two columns showing their simultaneously written diaries; Truffaut might have rendered the irony of the parallels and the

150

increasing divergencies between the diaries by using the split screen device. His emphasis on the vagueness behind many of the characters' decisions is illustrated by Claude's conclusion that he wishes to live alone, influenced by his reading of Nietzsche in the novel but less clearly motivated in the film (though Claude does talk of his decision to create books rather than children). More generally, Truffaut reverses his usual emphasis on the role of chance. Here what happens is largely the result of choice, even if the basis for it is often inadequate or irrational and reflects the characters' timidity and inexperience.

The final consummation of the Claude/Muriel relationship is condensed in the film into a rapidly narrated epilogue. Having earlier given Anne a romantic death from tuberculosis (influenced, he said, by the example of Emily Brontë), Truffaut thus avoids the novel's crueller, if less spectacular, reasons for the fading of Claude's relationship with Anne – Anne's happy marriage and four children, an unthinkable ending for Truffaut.

The predominantly literary emphasis of the film is balanced by Truffaut's attention to colour in his recreation of *la belle époque*. The contrast between the interiors and the exteriors, as in *Jules et Jim*, is even more powerfully illustrated here by the colours, which reflect the tones of the Impressionist canvases of the period. Truffaut enriched his study of the minutiae of desire, passion and tenderness with a happy marriage between words and images: a *Genou de Claire* filmed in delicate, sensual *and* functional tones.

Truffaut was 'increasingly tempted by films which combine literature and cinema . . . If *Fahrenheit 451* is a homage to all books, most of my films are homages to *a* book.' *Les Deux Anglaises et le Continent* endorses his view that 'if the beauty of a literary work lies in its prose, there is no reason not to let this prose be heard in the cinema'. The opening credits are superimposed over close-ups of the book cover, then one of the pages, several covers together, four covers on a shelf, then more pages, some annotated in the margin with Truffaut's shooting directions. A quotation from Claude's diary ('Muriel thought the account of our difficulties might help others') serves as a preface. The presence of the book will loom throughout, from this first moment until the last words.

The opening sequence, with quick cuts between Claude on the

swing, his mother and the upturned faces of the watching children (as at the puppet show in *Les Quatre Cents Coups*), establishes the closeness of the mother-son bond. The first meeting between Anne and Claude contrasts the formality and timidity of the spoken words with the revelation of Claude's thoughts as Anne raises her veil: 'I had the impression of a modest and agreeable nudity.' This is the first example of the commentary – sometimes narrated by Truffaut, here spoken by Claude reading from his diary – which enriches the whole film. It is the first intimation of what Roché called the 'total frankness' of the intimate diaries, which Truffaut faithfully reproduces. The interior of the Roc house – brocade curtains, pictures in heavy, ornate frames, aspidistras, solid furniture, rich carpets and a preponderance of strong, dark colours – creates an atmosphere of opulent comfort which seems to weigh upon the characters, inhibiting spontaneity and prompting a stifling formality. Claude's mother is a brooding presence, her influence over him captured in a close-up of her face superimposed over an aerial shot of the countryside traversed by a train (reminiscent of *Jules et Jim*), and the comment that she 'raised no objections' to his going to stay with the Brown family in Wales. (In the novel his mother goes too.)

The vivid green of the grass tracks, and the sunlight and shadow of the Welsh beach, contrast sharply with the claustrophobic gloom of the interior of the Browns' cottage. Here the heavy mahogany bannisters, the dark blue walls at the head of the stairs and in Claude's bedroom, and the deep grey curtains in the dining room, provide a fitting background for the solid British reserve of Mrs Brown and the near-silence of the first meal, punctuated only by polite banalities and Claude's awareness of the absence of Muriel. After her appearance the following day, when she peeps at Claude with a kind of demure coquetry from under the bandage which protects her strained eyes, she is shown resolving not to be jealous of her sister, though there has so far been no indication (as there is in the book) that she has any need to be. A further hint of the future two plus one breakdown of the trio, with each sister alternating as the odd one out, is seen in the long shot of Anne, on whom the iris closes, from the viewpoint of the other two above the cottage in the gorse, where Claude is correcting Muriel's French intonation.

Subsequent sequences reveal Claude's gradual assimilation into the family ('I feel I have been adopted by the two sisters'), and disturbing indications that his feelings for them are more than fraternal. The sea's luminous blue and the vivid green of the grass make up another sensual Impressionist backcloth against which the grey stone of the cottage and the light shades of the three tennis players' clothing are picked out. 'The three became inseparable,' but their moments of complete harmony are fleeting. During a parlour game, reminiscent of Antoine's mime of a private detective in *Baisers Volés*, Claude's forfeit is to perform the 'nun's kiss', i.e. through the bars of a chair, on Anne. Gentle, almost pastoral music swells on the soundtrack; the flames of the fire are reflected in Muriel's dark spectacles as she averts her gaze; Claude kisses Anne tenderly on the cheek, the two of them silhouetted in profile against the flames (a similar moment in *La Sirène du Mississippi* signifies love). Another 'innocent' game, *citron pressé* in a cave, awakens further strange stirrings in Claude as he is sandwiched between the 'elastic backs' of the sisters. Mrs Brown's termination of this activity prefigures her more consequential intervention later.

During Claude's walk with Muriel at night, at the masochistic instigation of Anne, their disagreement on the nature of love (for Claude it is physical, for Muriel there is only true love) is lightened by her offer, and his refusal, of the archetypal apple. The next shot of the women of the house singing as they iron, with the sea glistening white in the morning light, evokes specifically Degas' 'Les Repasseuses', and more generally the lyrical, pastoral tradition from Renoir (*père et fils*) to Widerberg. A midnight conversation during which Claude actually strokes Muriel's hand and cheek, and explains to her that he is doing so 'because you come from the earth', offends Mrs Brown's English sense of decorum. The effect of her admonishment of Claude, during which she refers to the future possibility of 'a stronger feeling' between Claude and Muriel, is ironically the exact opposite of her intentions.

The next scene is quintessential Truffaut. Strong, melodramatic music; rapid commentary reflecting the hero's tumultuous thoughts; a written declaration of love (cf. *Antoine et Colette* and *Baisers Volés*); visual representation of the passage of time between the delivery of the letter and the reply (successive shots of the Sacré Coeur in *Baisers Volés*, here a shot from Claude's viewpoint in a neighbour's cottage, to which he has been politely banished, of the

'I feel I have been adopted by the two sisters': Stacey Tendeter, Kika Markham and Jean-Pierre Léaud as *Les Deux Anglaises et le Continent*; (*below*) Muriel at her window

Browns' cottage by night, with one light burning, then by day, with Anne and Muriel together in the garden). The gap between what is said and what is felt is illustrated by Muriel's refusal, 'We are brother and sister. I will never be your wife,' Anne's disbelief in the permanence of Muriel's sentiments, and Muriel's own ringingly romantic declaration, when she is alone, of her love for Claude.

The film telescopes the transition between Muriel's 'no' and her 'perhaps'. The strength of her emotions ('I am like a river which swells and subsides' − with rolling waves in the background) is frustratingly repressed by Claude's subservience to his mother's opinion and the acceptance by the couple of the decision of their neighbour, called in as arbitrator, that they should separate for a year. The anguish of all three of them and the contending forces in play are symbolically conveyed in one lengthy shot panning from Claude and his mother on the right via Anne in the centre to Muriel weeping on her mother's shoulder on the left, then all in one movement back to Anne again, who in turn looks to her left. The actual moment of separation is like a death. Muriel even says, 'Imagine, one of us might have died.' Claude's train draws away noisily, like the sound of the crematorium furnace in *Jules et Jim*.

Claude's mother narrates her idyllic love for his father in another setting worthy of an Impressionist canvas: tea out of doors, parasols and flowery hats, reflections in a lake, the ripples of boats and oars, which slip out of focus and merge into a hazy light. The main emphasis during the separation is on Claude, mounting art exhibitions and enjoying sexual love, thanks especially to a warm-voiced, seductive painter, another Truffaut siren reminiscent of Fabienne Tabard. The one incident depicting Muriel during this time gains in impact from its isolation. Grainy shots of her playing tennis with Anne, interspersed with sudden strident chords of extraterrestrial music and blinding zooms into the sun, show her hallucination, vibrant with light, of Claude's face across the net. Claude's letter of renunciation, setting forth his vocation as a bachelor writer and alluding to his 'women friends', plunges Muriel into prolonged agonies of fainting and jealousy. She declares that she is his wife, sister and friend (shades of Antoine Doinel) whether he understands or not; she insists on absolute possession of Claude or nothing at all (like the 'stranger' in *Baisers Volés*); she has nightmares in the dark blue light of her bedroom (like those Louis has in *La Sirène du*

*Mississippi*). Finally, a shot through a rain-soaked window shows her in the dark blue interior with a white lamp, vowing to write her diary for herself and never to marry, removing her spectacles and rubbing her eyes (like Sabine in *Jules et Jim*). A shot of the two sisters painting out of doors, in which the background of the sea is faded rapidly from light blue to a velvety midnight hue, recalls the Monets and the other canvases of the period which Claude has just been examining.

Another scene, this time reminiscent of the paintings of Manet – a high-angle shot of an open-air café surrounded by dark green foliage and patterns of sun and shadow – shows Claude with his mother and then 'discovering' Anne as if for the first time. With Muriel no longer an obstacle, Claude's only battle is with himself. In Anne's studio 'the mad idea came to him of taking Anne's breast in his hand', and he does so. Stendhal would have approved and so does Anne. His excitement at being the first man to touch Anne leads to their decision to spend a few days beside a Swiss lake. An extract transposed from Muriel's letters in the novel ('Let us live. We'll put the label on afterwards') serves as an introduction to the longest and most poignant tracking shot in the film. In the same slow tempo as the lyrically swelling music, the camera moves gently from right to left, across trees and with water constantly in the foreground, picks up Anne carrying a ladder, loses her behind the foliage, moves at her pace along the face of the waterside shack and round the corner to encompass her and Claude, then continues on the left with Anne seen through reeds along the water's edge – all in one uninterrupted flow. Their pastoral idyll has begun.

Truffaut's habitual *pudeur* permeates the ensuing scenes of increasing intimacy. Like Tristan and Isolde, they undress the first night on either side of an improvised curtain and sleep separately. Next morning, Claude outside the shack is the pretext for the camera, inside, to follow him through a 180° arc, in which luxuriant squares of green foliage framed by the windows alternate with the total blackness of the interior, as he moves towards Anne sculpting outside. She wants to make statues, not babies; he calls her curiosity sacred and prophesies that she will have many men. 'Their kisses grew stronger.' The second night Anne learns that 'friends do not kiss each other on the lips with beating hearts', but her eagerness to lose her virginity is countered by her fear of doing so, and she sleeps quietly in Claude's arms. The third night, inspired by the flames of their log fire, Anne makes up her mind. The gentle humour of Claude's incredulous echoing of her decisions ('No curtain? No nightdress? No dress?') and her 'impossible red flannel underwear', gives way to tenderness as Claude asks her, naked in his bed, if she is really sure. As she draws to him, Truffaut slowly and discreetly fades to black and then equally slowly fades in the light. She has taken pleasure in his pleasure and in their intimacy, but 'it is not yet us'. Cut to a shot of the boathouse, landing stage, trees, shadows and deep blue of the lake, as Claude and Anne, silhouetted against the light, row away in separate boats. Claude wanted to prolong the idyll but Anne refused. 'They were free and it was beautiful.'

Three months later, when they meet again in Paris, Anne is in a state of wonder at her newfound womanhood: 'It was quite new for them both.' Anne is not jealous of Claude's other women, but strives to make an alternative life for herself, asking only, 'Love me as much as you can.' The comment that 'happiness is related with difficulty' anticipates the end of that happiness for Claude. Another lover enters Anne's life – a Russian publisher called Diurka – illustrated by a shot of Claude going upstairs to visit Anne (stairs feature prominently in Truffaut's films as the decor of many crises – Antoine in *Antoine et Colette*, and especially Christine in *Baisers Volés*). There is no reply to his knocks, and as Claude retraces his steps Truffaut fades to black. Next morning Claude tries to overcome his shock and manages to approve of Anne's actions, which are in accordance with their code; he advises her to go to Persia with Diurka and to listen only to the voice of her desire. Roché's succinct prose is heard in Claude's comment: 'Anne soon had two regular lovers. We both bore it badly. She, very well.' Then Truffaut's voice over: 'Before the departure for Persia, they had a farewell which lasted all night' (like the first kiss between Jim and Catherine in *Jules et Jim*).

The fortune-teller's prediction of unhappiness in love for Muriel, and a harmonious life with many men but with great danger for Anne, is followed by the arrival of a parcel for Claude containing Muriel's diary. Her intimate confession of shame at her habit of masturbation is spoken by her in a series of four intense close-ups, intercut with scenes illustrating the actions related. Claude is more curious than moved, regarding the whole account as potential material for a novel. His mother's death, conveyed visually, frees him from 'the most exclusive of all his women'. She lies in bed in a darkened room; suddenly very deep organ tones are heard, and the camera closes menacingly in on her; cut to a close-up of Claude wearing a black tie, and a background, which goes out of focus, of workmen removing a funeral drape from a building.

The film seems to gather momentum from this point. Claude sees Anne again in Paris, and then Muriel. He is frozen into inaction by his mental barriers: 'In Claude's thoughts Muriel was of a terrifying purity' (Truffaut's 'inviolate goddess' syndrome again). His confusion when *she* kisses *him* leads him to rush off in anguish, like Antoine in *Baisers Volés* after calling Fabienne 'Monsieur'. Muriel continues to take the initiative by inviting Claude to leave with her for the seaside. The repetition of Claude and Anne's decision that Muriel must be told about them, and Anne's protracted lingering over her account to her sister of her other two lovers, allows the audience to suffer in anticipation on Muriel's behalf. Her violent physical reaction to the knowledge that Claude is the third lover is accompanied by melodramatic music as she vomits and faints, the camera zooming in to the steps on which she strikes her head. Her letter of adieu is spoken by her in close-up, her weeping face superimposed over swiftly moving background shots of glittering water and trees.

Claude's own suffering is alleviated by his writing the story of his love for the two sisters. Its publication, as *Jérôme et Julien*, allows Truffaut to indulge his fascination for showing ponderous machinery (as in Louis' factory in *La Sirène du Mississippi*), here the manually operated printing press and the actual inking process. Claude's chance encounter (and such meetings are rare in this film) with Diurka, who works at the press, provides a moment of masculine complicity: they are both victims now. Like Truffaut (on his own admission) when he made the film, Claude now has 'the impression that it is the characters in the book who are going to suffer in (his) place'. Diurka accepts Claude's suggestion that the best way for him to find out why Anne broke off her engagement with a climber is to go and ask her, recalling the fairytale atmosphere of Jules and Jim's visit to the Greek statue and their resolution to follow any woman who looked like it.

The next shot, showing Diurka amid the green grass, the grey rocks and the pale blue waters of the Welsh estuary, is another Impressionist juxtaposition of complementary colours. Anne, who

Claude writes his love story

unbeknown to Diurka is dying of tuberculosis, agrees to be his, but a shot of her bedside medicine tray (like Louis' in *La Sirène du Mississippi*) is ominous. Diurka waits; the iris closes on Anne saying she will not now refuse to see a doctor; cut to a long shot of the cottage at night (recalling Claude's view of it much earlier) with one light burning. The light goes out, and the frame opens out from darkness with an iris shot of Diurka relating all this to Claude and adding Anne's terrifying phrase, 'My mouth is full of earth.'

Soon after, Muriel is met by Claude on the waterfront at Calais, to lyrical musical accompaniment. As the couple move off, the screen is filled with shimmering pale blue reflections of the water on the boat's gleaming black side. The eroticism of the climactic seduction of Muriel, willed by her, is unique in Truffaut. It is not so much that he finally succumbed to the general climate; indeed, what is actually shown even in this sequence is commendably discreet; but Truffaut said that rather than a film on physical love he wanted to make 'a physical film on love'. Hence the importance of the fainting,

159

vomiting, blood and tears. By comparison, in *Jules et Jim*, filmed at a distance in both space and time, the impact of the emotions is relatively diminished. Here the audience is made to experience the emotions with the characters, with a greater, almost physical immediacy. 'The violence of a love which has been for so long internal' wells up in Muriel. For Claude she is 'brand-new . . . aged thirty but looking like twenty . . . and he squeezed her like snow in his hands.' In contrast with the gentle tenderness of his first love encounter with Anne, here all is brutal passion as Claude unintentionally 'provides Muriel with a weapon to use against himself'. 'There was red upon her gold,' says Truffaut echoing Roché, and blood fills the screen. The rupture of Muriel's chastity is symbolic of the rupture of the ties that have bound her to Claude for seven years.

Next day she is dominant. She was resolved to come, see and conquer – 'I came to bury us.' Despite Claude's protests that she is now his wife, and his belated certainty that he loves her, she is now determined to leave. An 'amorous puritan' who is of a different race from Claude, she will not try to change him, nor will she stay with him, though she confesses, 'I can live without you as I can live without eyes or legs.' At the station two trains slowly cross in front of Claude and Muriel on the platform, each going in a different direction.

The epilogue, fifteen years later, relates that Mrs Brown is dead, and Muriel, married to a schoolteacher, has a daughter. A futile war has killed millions. Rodin's statue of Balzac, earlier praised by Claude, is now universally admired. Claude, bearded and bespectacled, walks in the garden of the Rodin museum and sees a party of English schoolgirls ('What if Muriel's daughter is among them?'). The camera circles the statue of 'Le Baiser'; Claude sees a reflection of his face and realizes he looks old; the film has depicted Roché's extraordinary love of life, but both Muriel and Anne have left Claude behind, and like Jules in *Jules et Jim* he is now alone. The final shot freezes on the stone doorposts and massive wooden door of the museum. We almost expect to hear Catherine singing again about the whirlwind of life.

# 17: Une Belle Fille Comme Moi

After his second variation on Roché's eternal triangle theme Truffaut switches the mood and doubles the parts for his next film *Une Belle Fille Comme Moi*. He returns to the one female against five males structure he had used in *La Mariée était en Noir*, in which Jeanne Moreau had waged her personal vendetta against the male sex. Just as in *Les Mistons* one woman – Bernadette Lafont as in this film – had proved impervious to the attentions of five adolescent boys. And we know that in Truffaut's universe men remain boys anyway, whatever their calendar age.

In *Belle Fille* Truffaut tries again to present the portrait of a bitch, having failed in *La Sirène du Mississippi* because he watered down his initial concept of the role of Catherine Deneuve. With Bernadette Lafont he had an actress who was certainly capable of playing the rumbustious, rollicking Moll Flanders role he had in mind. But ultimately her healthy vulgarity and aggressive sexuality are ill-served by Truffaut's customary lightweight, picaresque framework. Using her sex appeal to exploit a succession of male victims, she flits rather meaninglessly from one cardboard cut-out to the next without really disturbing anybody or anything.

Judged from an autobiographical point of view the film does offer insights into Truffaut's attempts to purge himself of the memory of his mother, as hinted at in the interview with the psychiatrist in *Les Quatre Cents Coups* and developed in *L'Homme qui Aimait les Femmes* and *L'Amour en Fuite*. But the disconnected ramblings of the analyst's couch constitute a tenuous and self-indulgent basis for a film, unless they are shaped into a coherent whole.

*Une Belle Fille Comme Moi*: Truffaut directing Bernadette Lafont

Unfortunately the film breaks very little new ground. There is no sense of excitement generated by a fresh insight or an extension of Truffaut's usual preoccupations. Rather, the impression is of stalemate. The territory is familiar in every sense – Truffaut at home surrounded by the family he has created in the safe universe peopled by his own inventions. Names recur; actors and actresses reappear; allusions to his own films proliferate (especially the attitudes to sexuality illustrated in *Tirez sur le Pianiste* and *La Mariée était en Noir*); Hitchcock's influence, here *Psycho* and *Vertigo*, is again acknowledged; autobiographical details, such as the Villejuif reformatory and the joke on the psychiatrist of *Les Quatre Cents Coups* (here transformed into a naïve sociologist), abound. But the mixture does not gell. All seems heavy-handed and contrived as Truffaut ransacks his previous films for formulae and ideas that have worked well in the past. But the free-wheeling approach which worked so well in *Tirez sur le Pianiste* and to some extent in *Baisers*

*Volés* fails here because Truffaut's touch and flair seem to desert him. There are many charming touches but *the* touch is lacking.

Stanislas, the young sociologist researching into female criminology, is the gentle, diffident male hero encountered in most of Truffaut's films. Arthur, the fumigation expert, is as complex-ridden about women and as fanatical a defender of the myth of their purity as the barman Plyne in *Tirez sur le Pianiste*, for whom all woman are 'pure, delicate, fragile, supreme and magical'. These attitudes to women are of course a running theme throughout Truffaut's entire work and they are repeated notably in *La Nuit Américaine* and *L'Homme qui Aimait les Femmes*. Other characters are equally predictable as, unfortunately, is the humour. What could have been the redeeming feature of the film fails because the jokes aren't funny, the knockabout fights and chases are too heavy and the comic business creaks.

Truffaut had reworked old themes in *Les Deux Anglaises*, but in a way that seemed enriching, so that at that point there was no need to think of new departures. As Muriel said to Claude, 'If you love someone, you love them as they are. You don't try to influence them. If you succeed, they will no longer be the same.' But the sterility of *Une Belle Fille Comme Moi* gave the lie to this optimism and raised doubts about Truffaut's capacity for development and renewal. Perhaps the kindest judgment on the film is to see it as a work of transition. It may be of interest to 'auteurists' but it can hardly sustain detailed scrutiny as a work of art in its own right. With hindsight Truffaut's tired recapitulation of his previously explored themes can now be seen as a necessary stopover point, allowing him to mark time and then gather his strength for the major lyrical masterpiece that is *La Nuit Américaine*.

# 18: La Nuit Américaine

Truffaut returns triumphantly to his best form with *La Nuit Américaine*. His total obsession with cinema finds its logical expression in this film about the making of a film. This is Truffaut's affectionate tribute to the cinema, a love song, a hymn to the crazy film industry and the eccentrics who work in it. Yet the film avoids eclecticism and conveys the impression of depicting, with warmth and intelligence, a surprisingly representative cross-section of humanity. Truffaut *en famille* again, surrounded by actors and film crew, makes us share his love of mankind like Renoir in *La Règle du Jeu*. Actors may be impossible but on or off the set they are constantly vulnerable, so they are also adorable and their whims are to be indulged. The message is again, as in *Baisers Volés*, that 'les gens sont formidables'.

In its freewheeling style and idiosyncratic tone, comprising Truffaut's quintessential tragi-comic mixture, the film recalls both *Baisers Volés* and *Tirez sur le Pianiste*. With its blend of humour and tenderness, it draws together both the 'American' and the 'French lyrical' strands in Truffaut's work. It is another Truffaut love story, another film in which the autobiographical thread is prominent. There is no division between the actors' lives and their work — and the actors here include Truffaut, virtually playing himself as the director of the film-within-the-film (his superb performance here as pacifier, cajoler and authority figure to his team of grown-up children recalls Dr Itard's handling of Victor in *L'Enfant Sauvage*, Truffaut's first major acting role), and Jean-Pierre Léaud, who may

*La Nuit Américaine*: 'A man who needs a wife, mistress, nurse and little sister all in one': Jean-Pierre Léaud with (*above*) Alexandra Stewart and (*below*) Dani

165

also be playing himself, torn between the conflicting demands of the cinema and his private life.

Truffaut's treatment of the dichotomy between real life and its mirror image on the screen, with constant overlapping and interplay between the two, is both moving and funny. The film-within-a-film device, of course, has many famous theatrical and cinematic antecedents, from the Corneille of *L'Illusion Comique* and the Molière of *L'Impromptu de Versailles* through Pirandello, Fellini and Godard. 'La Nuit Américaine', as the film explains, is the device of filming 'day for night', whereby night scenes are shot in daylight through a filter. It is typical of the cinematic tricks of the trade and illusion-creating devices which this film simultaneously exploits and exposes.

The dedication to Dorothy and Lillian Gish is the first of the many homages with which the film abounds. The opening sequence then creates the illusion of reality only to shatter it at once with the revelation that we are watching the shooting of a film, as Truffaut plays in his usual fashion with our expectations. The tragic development, interspersed with humour, of the film-within-the-film (*Meet Pamela*) is paralleled by similar vicissitudes in the lives of the people working on the film. The apprentice Script-Girl (Liliane), the Make-Up Girl (Odile), the Props Man (Bernard) are given equal prominence with the stars – Séverine, the fading Hollywood actress, Alexandre, her fifty-year-old husband in the film, their son Alphonse (Jean-Pierre Léaud) and their daughter-in-law Julie, who plays Pamela, who is in love with Alexandre.

The whole film is a demonstration that film-making, in the words of Truffaut, both the actor and the man, is 'un métier formidable'. He compares it to a journey in a Western. 'At first you hope you will have a good trip. Then you just wonder if you will ever reach the end.' And later: 'Films go on like trains. They are more harmonious than life and there are no hold-ups. Personal problems no longer count. The cinema reigns' – this to the accompaniment of majestically slow, swelling music.

The warmth and solidarity of the film-making team – they watch the rushes like a family watching home movies and later the group photograph resembles a family portrait – provides a temporary security for Truffaut. The importance of his craving is highlighted by the emphasis on the line 'Your parents invite us' (reminiscent of Antoine's adoptive family in *Antoine et Colette*). But the film also

166

stresses the isolation of the director in his decision-making, pater familias role. Hence his symbolic wearing of the hearing-aid and the recurrent enigmatic flashback (similar to an episode in *Les Quatre Cents Coups* and based on Truffaut's own experience) of a solitary child's theft of stills of *Citizen Kane* from outside a cinema, followed by flight into deafness.

The incident in which Séverine can't remember her lines and asks if she can just say numbers with the correct dramatic emphasis – 'as with Federico' – is followed by frequent reassurances from Truffaut that it is not serious. In her confusion Séverine cannot tell if Odile is her make-up girl or a film actress playing the part of the maid (in fact she's both). The sequence works on a number of levels. It is funny and moving; it is an authentic portrayal of Truffaut's working method, his delicate handling of actors and his sympathy for them; and it illustrates the confusion between illusion and reality which runs through the film.

Another thread running through this and other films of Truffaut is illustrated jocularly by Alphonse's question 'Are women magical?' (echoes especially of *Tirez sur le Pianiste* and *Baisers Volés*). The humorous and inconclusive responses vary from 'No, but some are exceptional' to 'No, but their legs are', until Julie tells him that 'Everyone is magical, or not' and then spends the night with him, like Fabienne Tabard in the shortlived idyll in *Baisers Volés*. The discretion and delicacy with which this scene is filmed contrasts with the boisterous good humour of the many other casual sexual encounters in the film. Alphonse is a continuation of the Antoine Doinel of *Domicile Conjugal*, significantly described by his girlfriend Liliane, who deserts him for a stuntman, as 'a moody, spoilt child who will never be a man' and who 'needs a wife, mistress, nurse and little sister' all in one.

Echoes of Catherine's 'whirlwind of life' song in *Jules et Jim* and an anticipation of Alexandre's death are contained in Séverine's observation 'Our life is funny. We meet; we work together; we make love and then – pouff, he is no longer there!' The sadness increases with Julie's remorse at Alphonse's revelation to her husband of her infidelity and her decision to live alone since 'life is disgusting'. The moment of muted optimism in the reconciliation with her husband is painfully mirrored (on the set) by Truffaut, following his routine of drawing upon actual conversation to form the basis of the next day's

167

On set: Jean-Pierre Léaud, Jacqueline Bisset and Truffaut as the director

Illusion and reality: Valentina Cortese as Séverine, Jean-Pierre Aumont as Alexandre, Nike Arrighi as Odile

169

Jean-Pierre Léaud and François Truffaut in *La Nuit Américaine*

script. As Alphonse gently touches her nose by candlelight and assures her that life is not disgusting, the shattering news arrives of Alexandre's death in a car crash.

These events, as always in Truffaut's films, overshadow the ending; and, as usual, he tries to lighten the mood. The film is hastily terminated with Alphonse shooting Alexandre's double in the back, in a scene reminiscent of *Tirez sur le Pianiste*, involving a revolver twirling amidst snow (here produced artifically by machine) to fast musical accompaniment. Odile, who 'has known many men', and one of the camera crew, 'who has known few women', announce their marriage, but our memory of the unhappy relationship between Jules and Catherine in *Jules et Jim*, about whom the same words were used, colours our amusement. The film unit breaks up and the camera pulls up and away from the scene of their farewells, the final shot freezing and then spinning round, evoking yet again the whirlwind – or the merry-go-round? – of life.

# 19: L'Histoire d'Adèle H.

After the spectacular synthesis of his earlier themes in the cele-
bratory *La Nuit Américaine* it was difficult to see where Truffaut
could go next. In fact he decided to take a break from film-making
to allow time for writing and the gestation of new projects. When
he had previously taken a similar decision, he had kept it for little
more than a year before returning to the cinema to make *Les Deux
Anglaises et le Continent*. On this occasion he was more successful
and it was not until two years later that he made his next film,
*L'Histoire d'Adèle H.*

In its concentration on the leading character, played by Isabelle
Adjani in her first major role, and the obsessive nature of her
emotions, the film anticipates the sombre intensity of *La Chambre
Verte* – that other piece scored for solo instrument. Yet it also
harks back to the two-sister theme of *Les Deux Anglaises*, in which
Muriel could not achieve happiness with Claude because of his
earlier affair with her elder sister, Anne, who had since died. It has
been noted that a clue to Truffaut's fascination with this theme
may be seen in his cinematic and real-life relationships – as *La
Nuit Américaine* indicates, for Truffaut the distinction between the
two is frequently blurred – with the two sisters Françoise Dorléac
and Catherine Deneuve. Miss Dorléac starred in *La Peau Douce*
and later met a violent death. Miss Deneuve starred in *La Sirène*,
then in *Le Dernier Métro* and became, according to Truffaut's frequent co-scriptwriter Bernard Revon, 'the most beautiful love of
his life'.

The link between the two-sister theme and *L'Histoire d'Adèle H.*

'. . . the moth being consumed by the flame'

Adèle (Isabelle Adjani) becomes a spy and a voyeur

may not be immediately apparent until it is realized that Adèle laboured under two enormous burdens. The first is that she was the daughter of Victor Hugo, who was, in Gide's famous 'bon mot', 'the greatest French poet of the nineteenth century – alas!' and Truffaut has admitted that he was attracted by the fact that Adèle was the daughter of the most celebrated man in the world. Great men usually cast cold shadows, in which nothing much grows, or at least not without a great struggle. The other cross borne by the wretched Adèle was the family drama which occurred when she was thirteen. Her elder sister Léopoldine was tragically drowned in the Seine at the age of nineteen, along with her young husband who had tried to rescue her. This event plunged Adèle's father into mourning, engulfed him in bitterness and led to his treating his surviving daughter, whom he had always favoured less than her elder sister, with increasing coldness. Léopoldine's dress was afforded the status of religious relic and she herself was elevated to sainthood by her father. So Adèle was the bearer of a double burden.

She entrusted her innermost thoughts to a voluminous, coded diary, which came to light only in the late Sixties, when Frances Vernor Guille, an American researcher, published her transcription. Truffaut had come across it in 1969 and determined to film it. His collaborator was again Jean Gruault, as for *L'Enfant Sauvage* – based upon another authentic case history – and for *Les Deux Anglaises* – which was again originally a personal diary. The film was written over a period of five years during which Truffaut made three other films – all of which constituted a quite typical working pattern for him.

The reduction of Adèle's surname to the letter H is indicative of her attempt to escape from the weight of the family name. She needs to assert her own personality and her right to her own individual existence. If *L'Enfant Sauvage* illustrates the struggle to acquire an identity and integration into society, then *Adèle H.* illustrates the reverse process with Adèle refusing her ready-made, spurious identity and moving beyond the outer rim of society to a point where notions of identity have no meaning.

Adèle's resistance finds expression in the most romantic, intransigent, absolute and hopeless love, which leads her through scandal and humiliation into madness. Her doomed and pathetic

Adèle in her terrifying solitude

genius – she is indeed her father's daughter – is revealed in her headstrong rebellion, belief in the power of the supernatural, vivid imagination and a stubborn capacity to go all the way at whatever cost. She shares with Julie in *La Mariée*, the stranger in *Baisers Volés*, and Julien in *La Chambre Verte* an all-consuming obsessive vision which she pursues with the relentlessness of Greek tragedy. Another of Truffaut's portraits of the absolute and definitive in a world which is full of the temporary and the provisional.

Adèle is also consumed by the 'demon of literature'. Truffaut, to whom literature was as much his lifeblood as cinema, delights as always in showing on the screen the palpable physical presence of written material in the shape of letters, diaries and press extracts. Adèle's famous father, who is never seen in the film, continues to exercise his hold over her, behaving like a rich bourgeois anxious to preserve both his international reputation and his financial control of his daughter. So we are again in authentic Truffaut territory with the problem of the relationship with the father, the

174

'Adèle . . . in pursuit of the impossible love by which she will be destroyed'. Isabelle Adjani with Bruce Robinson

importance of a name, the link between the name and the personality and the quest for an identity all looming large.

Adèle erupts predictably from this environment in pursuit of the impossible love by which she will be destroyed. The seed of pain and grief that was germinated in the heart of Antoine Doinel when his love for Colette was not reciprocated, comes to a full and terrible fruition in the anguished sufferings of Adèle H. The film is totally centred on her and her terrifying solitude to the extent of becoming almost a monologue. Indeed so obsessed is Truffaut with the performance of Adjani that he virtually neglects the awkwardness and stilted English dialogue of the supporting characters. As in *Fahrenheit 451* and *Les Deux Anglaises*, these performances are disturbingly inept, even more than usual for a director working in a foreign language.

Adèle's 'amour fou' fixation is even more pathetic in that the

175

Truffaut in a brief Hitchcockian appearance, and Adèle (Isabelle Adjani)

object of her passion is an unworthy and feckless libertine. He is a young English lieutenant, Albert Pinson, whom Adèle met during one of her father's table-turning séances in Guernsey. She probably became his mistress and marriage may have been discussed. His regiment is transferred to Nova Scotia and the film begins with Adèle's arrival in Halifax in hot pursuit. Henceforth she devotes all her energy and ingenuity to one end – marriage to her beloved, who shows nothing but indifference to her. She lies, deceives, becomes a spy and a voyeur and offers Pinson the present of a prostitute, all to no avail. She even inserts notices of their marriage in the papers. To Pinson she has become a total embarrassment. He wants nothing more than to be left alone to his simple lusts. Yet she surely sees herself as a female Hernani. She is frequently shown against a background of the sea, exactly like her father in his role as famous romantic exile.

Adèle's trailing of Pinson continues over several years ending with her down and out in Barbados and in dire straits. Her quest has become an object in itself. When she finally passes Pinson in the street in Bridgetown, the irony is that she does not even recognize or hear him. The final commentary informs us that she is shipped back to her father, who is now widowed, and spends the last forty years of her life in asylums. Her father dies in 1885 with the words, 'I see a dark light.' Adèle is condemned to live on for thirty more years before slipping almost unnoticed 'into that good night', having first found release by descending into the encroaching darkness of madness years earlier. Truffaut has again won his bet by getting us to share his own fascination and obsession, akin to the 'sterile curiosity' of Dr Itard in *L'Enfant Sauvage*, as we watch the moth being consumed by the flame.

# 20: L'Argent de Poche

'And now for something completely different,' Truffaut may well have cried as, with scarcely a pause for breath, he plunged into his next film *L'Argent de Poche*. Not for the first time he felt the need to make a film in complete contrast to the previous one. So he moves from the intensive focusing on the inner turmoil of one character in *Adèle H.* to a more relaxed, seamless and even random series of near-sketches about childhood. More than any other of his films, the success of *L'Argent de Poche* depends on the extent to which the spectator shares, or comes to share, the director's viewpoint, namely here that childhood is a 'state of grace'.

The starting point for the film occurred as far back as the late Fifties, when Truffaut was filming *Les Quatre Cents Coups*. His original idea was that the action would take place entirely within the classroom and that the film would dispense with conventional narrative. It then developed into a project to make a film about a lot of children without highlighting any one of them. But what the film eventually becomes is something altogether more conventional with two children emerging from the ruck to embody many of the attitudes already seen in the Doinel cycle and *L'Enfant Sauvage*.

The film was shot over a period of two months in the small town of Thiers. Truffaut seeks to impose a semblance of unity, if not order, on the disparate succession of episodes and improvizations culled from a variety of sources by adhering more or less, as in *La Nuit Américaine*, to the unities of time and place. But Truffaut's view of childhood is excessively rose-tinted and sentimental, sometimes bordering on the arch and the twee. The

'Liaisons Dangereuses' at the cinema. (Truffaut's second daughter, Ewa)

Childhood – 'a state of grace?'

children in the film figure in a series of anecdotes, some solemn, some light and whimsical, but all of them heavy with the voice of Truffaut warning of the moral implications of neglecting children or even of treating them with anything less than his own rather benevolent indulgence.

The children in question attend the local school and benefit from teachers endowed with more humane and understanding attitudes than the tyranical bullies at whose hands Antoine Doinel suffered. Their parents range from respectable flat-dwellers to cosy shop-keepers, from a soft-spoken, paralysed father who sits alone with his books, whose pages are turned for him by machine, to a screaming outcast of a mother who lives in a sort of toolshed into which her son, a late arrival at the school, has to climb by ladder. This structure allows Truffaut to introduce characters and episodes at will just as in *Domicile Conjugal*.

The exercise is unfortunately never less than uneasy and is not helped by the fact that one of the earliest episodes is the most fatuous of all: Baby Gregory in pursuit of the family cat crawls out over the ninth-floor balcony and launches into space – only to land unscathed in the bushes below. Moral – 'Children are tough and . . . there's a providence that looks after them,' says a Truffaut surrogate, a theme that will be developed later in the film.

'A film is not a settling of old scores,' as Truffaut tells himself in the Doinel series and elsewhere, only to spend a large part of his oeuvre and certainly of this film in doing exactly that. In this portrait of childhood from birth to adolescence Truffaut fills in some of the pieces that were missing in the jigsaws of *Les Mistons* and *Les Quatre Cents Coups*. The effect of childhood having been for him 'a bad time to get through' leads him to be temperamentally unable to bear the sight of children suffering and undermines the objectivity and credibility of the film's plea for children's rights.

The segment of the film involving Patrick is the most developed and allows Truffaut most scope for the reworking of old themes. Patrick's father is confined to a wheelchair and as such condemned to being fairly ineffective as was Antoine's father (emasculated for different reasons) in *Les Quatre Cents Coups*. The missing or ineffective father is commonplace throughout Truffaut's films and is certainly linked with Truffaut's doubts about his own

Patrick & Martine begin their rites of passage into adulthood

origins and uncertainty as to who his father was. Other echoes from the Doinel cycle occur when Patrick and his friend take a couple of girls to the cinema and Patrick's inexperience with girls is shown up, just as in *Antoine et Colette*. He then falls hopelessly in love with his friend's large blonde mother, in an episode again reminiscent of *Antoine et Colette* and especially of *Baisers Volés*.

The other episode showing Truffaut's personal themes surviving intact concerns the battered child Lucien from the toolshed home. Truffaut's most powerful depiction of a suffering 'wild' child was of course in *L'Enfant Sauvage*. The resemblance between Lucien's mute, sullen figure and the noble potential of the 'savage' are obvious and represent a distillation of all Truffaut's retrospective fears for himself.

The speech by the schoolteacher near the end voices the film's over-explicit moral. Unhappy adults can always defend themselves. Children cannot. A battered child always feels guilty, so parents who beat children are always odious. The reverse side of the medal is that a tough childhood often produces a resilient adult who is able to cope in a tough world. The heaviness of the message is then lightened by the final sequence showing two of the adolescents, Patrick and Martine, exchanging a kiss that has been set up by their jeering friends at the summer holiday camp. Their rites of passage into adulthood have begun.

# 21: L'Homme qui Aimait les Femmes

It is an open question whether Bertrand Morane in *L'Homme qui Aimait les Femmes* is much further advanced along the road to adulthood than Patrick in *L'Argent de Poche*. In this context Bernard's revelation, having advertised for a baby-sitter, that the baby is in fact himself, is quite significant. But the understandable accusations of male chauvinism that greeted the film's release are not fully substantiated, as a closer reading of the text reveals.

What Truffaut gives us here is another portrayal of a man gripped by an obsession – in this case the obsession is women, and in particular women's legs. As with most recent studies of the Don Juan of literature and legend, he is presented as almost a clinical case, unable to help himself, more victim than victor. This interpretation is supported by the fact that the vast numbers of women that pass through his hands bear him no grudge but actually feel warmth and affection for him, an unlikely reaction were he simply to have manipulated them for his own ends. Which is why they arrive in such numbers at his funeral, with which the film opens.

Their legs, seen from the imagined eyeview of Bertrand in the grave, are 'compasses that bestride the globe'. Charles Denner's performance recalls his previous roles for Truffaut – as Fergus, the seducer 'seduced', in *La Mariée était en Noir* and as Arthur, the obsessive rat-catcher, in *Une Belle Fille Comme Moi*. Bertrand's 'special way of asking – as if his life depended on it' is the reason for his success with women. His remedy when he is refused – by a woman of his own age who prefers younger men – is in time-honoured Truffaut style to write his autobiography. The book has

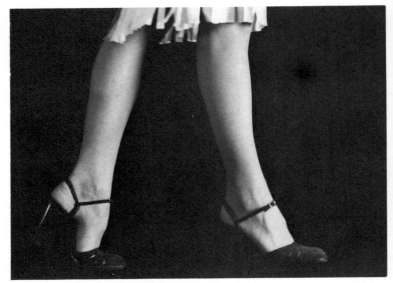

'compasses that bestride the globe'

'Bertrand prefers the protection of a multiplicity of encounters'

184

'... a case of arrested development ... men are little boys eternally playing childish games'

the same title as the film, thus affording much scope for flashbacks and voiceovers, echoing the film-within-the-film device of *La Nuit Américaine* and anticipating *L'Amour en Fuite*.

Truffaut prefaced his 'book-of-the-film' with a significant quotation from Bruno Bettelheim regarding accession to adulthood: 'Being reborn, being capable of emotions, and even desiring to be loved do not constitute a fully human existence. There is a further need – to be able to be active, to be able deliberately to hold out one's hand to the other for warmth and affection, to be able to dare to bridge the gap between the self and the other, to hold out one's hand and transform the physical separation between two bodies into an intimacy, to love and not simply to love being loved.'

Flashback showing Bertrand's mother treating her adolescent son (Michel Marti) 'as if he were sexually neutral or even non-existent'

For Bertrand such a rebirth is impossible. He is too obsessed with himself to be able to perceive the other. A constant procession of others have entered his bed without his ever having known them in any but the biblical sense.

His encounter with Vera, played by Leslie Caron, failed because this essential perception, this knowledge of the other, never took place. 'We didn't tell each other the same story,' says Vera, when they meet five years later. Bertrand was incapable of knowing Vera because he never knew himself. Like Antoine Doinel he is constantly in search of his identity, which he only begins to discover in the course of the film – by writing his autobiography. He is now free to move on from the stage of mere sexual curiosity: 'What else have all these women got that all the ones I know don't have? That's just it! What they have is that they are unknown.' In theory he can now start to recognize love. In practice he still prefers a fantasy of love and the protection of a multiplicity of encounters. As Fabienne tells him: 'Not merely do you not want love, you

Truffaut on the set of *L'Homme qui Aimait les Femmes* with Geneviève Fontanel 'the woman who prefers younger men'

even refuse to be loved. You think you like love, but it's not true, you merely like the idea of love!' And he is unable or unwilling to find the incarnation of that love in one woman. After his death Geneviève notes: 'Bertrand sought an impossible happiness in quantity, in the multitude.' Every woman he meets is desired, but not loved, by him, as his idea of love is nothing more than a sort of multifragmented desire. As Geneviève says: 'For my part there is no doubt that he loved them all in his own way . . . They are all different. Each one has something the others don't have, something unique and irreplaceable' – shades of Delphine Seyrig's speech in *Baisers Volés*! The love of Bertrand, like that of Antoine, is child-like, immature and provisional. Like Claude Roc, he messes up the crucial encounter of his life – with Vera – and he dies before his relationship with the loving and understanding Geneviève has time to develop.

The key to Bertrand's behaviour is provided by flashback sequences. These show his sexual initiation by a young prostitute – similar to the account in *Les Quatre Cents Coups*, except that in

'His remedy when he is refused . . . is to write his autobiography'

Antoine's case the girl never showed up – and they reveal the mental association for Bertrand between the prostitute and his mother. She has numerous lovers and keeps lists of their names in a drawer. She also walks up and down in front of the adolescent Bertrand, just like Gilberte in front of Antoine in *Les Quatre Cents Coups*, as if he were sexually neutral or even non-existent (as both adolescents would have been if their respective mothers' abortion attempts had succeeded). Antoine suffers similarly dismissive treatment at the hands of Colette, who in many ways mirrors his mother's rejection of him and also her coldness and inaccessibility. In *L'Homme qui Aimait les Femmes* the result is Bertrand's need to divide women into fragments, with a particular obsession for their legs, and his consequent failure to see them as whole people. Further evidence for the idea of Bertrand as a case of arrested development is to be found in the job that he performs – he is an engineer in charge of model planes and boats. As in *Domicile Conjugal* and *La Femme d'à Côté* men are seen as through the eyes of women, as little boys eternally playing childish games.

Structurally the film does not entirely avoid the danger of becoming a mere catalogue of couplings, or more properly of events preceding and succeeding couplings, since Truffaut still prefers suggestion to revelation in sexual matters. Typically and frustratingly Truffaut runs away from the tragic dimension of this portrait of a blocked personality locked unhappily into obsessive solitude. The tone is persistently light, the mood is exuberant and the comic encounters are very funny indeed. But the underlying sadness of a film that opens and closes in the Saint-Lazare cemetery, where Truffaut himself was to be buried some seven years later, cannot really be concealed and with hindsight it gives the film a special poignancy.

# 22: La Chambre Verte

If Truffaut veers away from the tragic dimension in *L'Homme qui Aimait les Femmes*, he certainly meets it head on in *La Chambre Verte*, whose subject is the most difficult he ever undertook. Even to consider making a film about death and fidelity to the memory of the dead represents a considerable act of courage within the framework of the commercial cinema. But Truffaut with his concept of a film as 'a bet to be won' accepted the challenge and made the film – which became an outstanding critical success and a resounding commercial failure.

Some ten years after the First World War Julien Davenne – played by Truffaut himself – is living quietly in a small town in eastern France where he writes the Deaths column in the local newspaper. He feels guilty at having escaped unscathed from a war that killed or mutilated so many young men. He is also a man with a secret in his life – again we see the influence of Hitchcock, though the particular source of inspiration for this film is to be found in two short stories by Henry James, *The Altar of the Dead* and *The Beast in the Jungle*. His secret is his veneration for his wife Julie, who had died shortly after their marriage – shades of Léopoldine in *Adèle H*. Julien meditates on her memory and communicates with her in his shrine – the 'Green Room' consecrated to her in his house.

His chance encounter with Cécilia, an auctioneer's assistant – played by Nathalie Baye – leads to the revelation that something extraordinary happened when they first met fifteen years earlier – they both experienced the sensation of the appearance of a loved

'Julien, another portrait in Truffaut's gallery of 'definitive' characters'

one at the very moment of that person's death thousands of miles away. The second link between them is a person. Julien loves all the dead *except* this one person; Cecilia loves all the dead but *especially* this one person, despite having once suffered greatly at his hands.

Contrary to established social and religious conventions, Truffaut's thesis is that it is just as possible to maintain vital and passionate relationships with the dead as with the living. Should the dead be forgotten? Does one have a right, or even a duty, to 'remake one's life'? Truffaut again depicts the violence of emotions and in particular the struggle between the definitive and the provisional, even if definitive commitment extends beyond the grave, a development of the theme treated extensively throughout his work.

The film strikes another note typical of Truffaut in its depiction yet again of a character gripped by an obsession – in this case the need to preserve the memory of the dead. The visual representation

191

'Julien loves all the dead except this one person'

of their memory is in the form of flaming candles, symbolic of the continuity of life. From the shrine to Balzac in *Les Quatre Cents Coups*, the burning books in *Jules et Jim* and *Fahrenheit 451*, the use of fires in *La Sirène* and *Les Deux Anglaises*, the candle in *L'Enfant Sauvage* and finally the forest of flaming candles in *La Chambre Verte*, flames never failed to exercise a powerful and almost primeval fascination over Truffaut and to provide a leit-motif throughout his work.

Another familiar theme, the triangle, is again present in *La Chambre Verte*, though perhaps less obviously than elsewhere. Julie may be dead but her absent body is paradoxically highly present in the images and objects – photographs, jewellery, a plaster hand – that Julien has kept as mementoes of her, not to mention the life-size dummy of his wife that he has had made. The necrophiliac implications are clear, though never developed, as Julien seeks to rediscover his wife's physical presence, only to be repeatedly con-fronted by her absence. Cécilia, to continue the paradox, is more

Julien (François Truffaut), Cécilia (Nathalie Baye) and 'the forest of flaming candles'

of a spiritual presence to Julien than a woman of flesh and blood. Julien gradually progresses from the physical, tangible object, in the shape of the dummy of his dead wife, to her symbolic representation in the shape of the candle flame. He is in a state of movement away from the flesh and towards the spirit, but he dies before he can finally complete the transition. 'You love the dead in opposition to the living,' says Cécilia, '. . . for you to love me, I would have to be dead.' Her own emotions are less obsessive and more balanced: 'I love and respect the dead but I also love the living.'

The object of Julien's desire is dead and the intensity of his emotions is in danger of leading him into madness. So obsessed is he with the absent Julie that he is not merely unable to respond to the love of Cécilia: it is as if he hardly even notices what she is offering. It is Julie who continues to exercise a powerful hold on Julien and to draw him inexorably towards death. In *La Chambre Verte* carnality is associated with the dead and spirituality with

193

the living and Julien cannot free himself from his desire for the dead Julie. A telling sequence in Julien's private chapel shows Cécilia moving towards the portrait of Julie above the altar. A close-up of Cécilia is then juxtaposed with Julie's portrait and a note in the script points out: 'The spectator may be struck by the idea that the two rivals are face to face. Cécilia looks the dead woman in the eyes and we have the impression that we are witnessing a confrontation between life and death.' Julie wins the battle and Cécilia's 'I love you' is too late to prevent Julien from dying. All she can do is to transform her love into light and the realm of the spirit as she weepingly lights the last candle for Julien. Another triangle has been sundered, again leaving at the end, as in *Jules et Jim* and *Les Deux Anglaises*, an isolated individual condemned to absolute solitude.

Julien is another portrait in Truffaut's gallery of 'definitive' characters. He remains unswervingly faithful to his love: 'I decided that, even if for others she was dead, to me she would always be alive.' He advises his bereaved friend: 'Don't think that you have lost her. Rather think that now you can never lose her again. Dedicate all your thoughts to her, all your actions, all your love.' Julien chooses light and the flames of countless candles to celebrate his love for Julie and the rest of his dead. The irony is that, the more faithful he is to his absolute ideal, the more he sinks into the closed world of the dead: 'I want to do more for her, to construct a permanent sanctuary where she will shine brightly, an altar of light where she will be the central flame.'

The object of Julien's love becomes imperceptibly part of his cult of death. The only things left of Julie, 'the eternally young woman', are objects – the photographs, the portraits, the ring, the plaster hand – fetishistically preserved in the Green Room, as in a sanctuary or a tomb. After the purifying fire has destroyed the Green Room, Julien transfers his objects to the private chapel he has acquired and progresses from concentration on objects to concentration upon the symbol of those objects, the candle flame. Julien becomes the first of Truffaut's 'definitive' characters to die. His brand of absolutism has led to his virtual suicide. As the doctor says: 'You can't heal someone who has lost the will to live.' Cécilia's desolation recalls that of Jules at the end of *Jules et Jim* who 'would no longer have the fear that he had had from the first day, firstly that

Catherine would deceive him and then simply that she would die, since it had now happened.' (Hamlet's 'If it is now, it is not to come'.) Jules can no longer lose Catherine.

Truffaut's confidence in himself and his ability to tackle difficult themes grows almost film by film, as he reveals progressively more of himself. In *La Chambre Verte* he acted for the third and last time in a major role in one of his own films. 'I appear in *La Chambre Verte* so that the film can be more intimate . . . Just as, when I do my mail in the office, I dictate some letters for typing and I write others by hand. *La Chambre Verte* is like a hand-written letter. It won't be perfect, it may be a little shaky, but it will be you, your handwriting.' At the age of forty-six Truffaut had realized that half the cast of *Tirez sur le Pianiste* were dead and many of his friends' names had been erased from his personal address book for the same reason. He no longer felt the need to hide behind somebody else's words to talk about death or any other deeply felt experiences. His work is now written, more confidently and powerfully than ever, in the first person.

# 23: Le Dernier Métro

True to his practice of alternating the serious with the light, Truffaut made *L'Amour en Fuite*, another first person statement and the final episode in the Antoine Doinel cycle, in the same year – 1978 – that he finished *La Chambre Verte*. He then began the preparation of *Le Dernier Métro*, which was conceived as the second part of a trilogy comprising *La Nuit Américaine* and a final film, *L'Agence Magic*, about the music-hall, one of the unfinished projects on the drawing-board at the time of his death in 1984 – see Chapter 26.

*Le Dernier Métro*, set in Paris during the Second World War, came in the wake of a spate of substantial French films on the subject of the war and the Occupation, ranging from Melville's *L'Armée des Ombres* to Ophuls' *Le Chagrin et la Pitié*, Malle's *Lacombe Lucien*, Costa-Gavras' *Section Spéciale* and Losey's *Mr Klein*. For years the war had been a taboo subject in France with painful memories of the Occupation, routine anti-semitism, censorship and French collaboration still fresh in people's minds. In comparison with such illustrious predecessors Truffaut's treatment of the subject seems lightweight, the Occupation being little more than a backcloth to the central drama of a theatrical troupe striving to survive despite the atmosphere of repression and persecution. Just as in *Baisers Volés*, filmed in 1968 when the collapse of the French state appeared imminent, Truffaut's interest in the major events of the day is so peripheral that they are almost reduced to the level of local colour. One feels that his main concern at any time of national crisis, if he were in the middle of making a film,

Nadine (Sabine Haudepin, the little girl in *Jules et Jim*) and Bernard (Gérard Depardieu)

'Truffaut's homage to Catherine Deneuve'

Bernard (Gérard Depardieu), Marion (Catherine Deneuve) and Lucas (Heinz Bennent)

would have been frustration at not being able to finish the film. The creative artist's myopic egotism reflects the tunnel vision shown by the Théâtre Montmartre company in *Le Dernier Métro*. The theatre 'reigns supreme', just like the cinema in *La Nuit Américaine*. The only principle to command support, as if it were a self-evident truth, is: 'the show must go on'.

Truffaut at least has the merit of consistency in refusing yet again to treat large-scale political or social subjects, preferring merely to show the repercussions of major events on individual human behaviour. In *Le Dernier Métro* Truffaut seems to take pains to protect his characters from suffering too much, despite touching on the problems of antisemitism, the Resistance, the black market, collaboration and survival. They talk about suffering in the play they are rehearsing and performing but emerge relatively unscathed themselves. The explanation for this may lie, as so often, in the autobiographical dimension. During the Occupation Truffaut was a young adolescent, no older than Antoine in *Les Quatre Cents*

'Yes, love hurts . . .' (Depardieu & Deneuve)

*Coups*, and *Le Dernier Métro* sometimes seems more like a child's view of events. Truffaut said as much himself in 1983.

In a world torn apart by war the theatre is all that counts for Marion Steiner, who assumes responsibility as both director and leading lady of the Théâtre Montmartre in Paris, after her husband Lucas, who is a Jew, has ostensibly fled the country. We learn that Lucas before the war only read the entertainments page in the newspaper, an admission Truffaut once made of himself. Writing to the cast of *Le Dernier Métro* in January 1980 just before filming began, Truffaut states categorically that in the film 'the characters are more important than the situations', rather as if he were re-affirming a fundamental principle for the whole of his work. As in *La Chambre Verte* the importance of the war is limited to its impact on human relationships and what it reveals of the strengths and weaknesses of the characters. Truffaut concentrates on individuals at the expense of any ideological, social or political considerations. In *Le Dernier Métro* there is no interest in the collective dilemma, no study of a group of people united by a common despair. The

199

title of the film is in fact a rather gratuitous allusion to one element of the general climate of oppression during the Occupation. A voice-over informs us that because of the eleven p.m. curfew in Paris all entertainments have to finish early enough to allow audiences and performers to catch the last metro home. The metro never actually figures in the film but there is what could be called an 'underground' dimension in that Lucas Steiner, the Jewish theatre director, who is supposed to be in exile abroad, is in fact in hiding quite literally underground. From the cellars under the stage he listens to rehearsals through an air vent and manages to direct the play clandestinely at one remove.

The members of the theatrical company illustrate the whole range of attitudes to life under the Occupation. At one extreme Bernard Granger, the new leading man – played by Gérard Depardieu – continues the 'underground' theme as an active undercover member of the Resistance. At the other the soubrette Nadine – played by Sabine Haudepin, who was the little girl in *Jules et Jim* and *La Peau Douce* – shows single-minded dedication in the pursuit of her career, even if it means fraternizing with German officers. The rest of the troupe survive as best they can within the hermetic world of the theatre, looking no further than the next performance. As Truffaut says in his 1983 introduction to the definitive script, homosexuals and Jews were equal targets for Nazi persecution: 'The fascist critics regularly denounced "the Jew-ridden plays of Bataille and the effeminate plays of Cocteau".' So Truffaut incorporates sequences referring to both these elements in *Le Dernier Métro*. Unfortunately the atmosphere of indulgent humanism in which all the characters bathe is redolent of the catch-all 'people are wonderful', 'everybody has his reasons' mood of *Domicile Conjugal*, itself but a pale reflection of Renoir's *Le Crime de Monsieur Lange*. In his determination to be non-judgmental Truffaut does not altogether avoid the danger of being merely charming. Even the villain of the piece, the collaborationist theatre critic Daxiat, is given redeeming features. He pursues his rabid anti-semitism with such unremitting zeal as to qualify for a place in Truffaut's gallery of compulsive obsessives. His behaviour, if never condoned, is at least illumined by his claim 'I adore the theatre, I live for the theatre but theatre people detest me,' a feeling perhaps dredged subconsciously from Truffaut's memories of reactions to

'You are so beautiful, to look at you is to suffer' (Deneuve & Depardieu)

his own brand of passionate and often vituperative film criticism in the Fifties. The character of Daxiat is based on an episode related by Jean Marais in his autobiography, where he recalls how he beat up the critic of *Je Suis Partout*, Alain Lambeaux, for his review of Cocteau's *La Machine Infernale*. The role proved a perfect cameo part for Jean-Louis Richard, who had worked with Truffaut before both as actor, co-writer and co-producer.

Above all, *Le Dernier Métro* is Truffaut's homage to Catherine Deneuve, who overturns her icy femme fatale stereotype with her suberb performance as the mature, responsible Marion Steiner. Marion is at the apex of another Truffaldian triangle and alternates between calculating charm, coolness and repressed passion, while also hesitating between Lucas and Bernard, just as Catherine hesitated between Jules and Jim. She copes with the exigencies of the tripartite situation by never making a final choice between the two men. At the end of the film she is shown centre stage as the camera pans from her holding the hand of her husband to the other hand holding that of her lover. The camera has resolved the problem visually by flattening out the triangle into a straight line. On – or 'in' – the one hand the 'definitive' Lucas who understands his wife, knows she is torn between himself and Bernard and is prepared to do anything to keep her. On the other the 'provisional' Bernard, whose strength of allegiance to Marion is unclear, has certainly demonstrated the strength of the sexual attraction. At the end of the film the problem is not resolved, merely postponed.

The artificial nature of the denouement is typical of the play on sentiment and artifice that runs through the film. The actors have been rehearsing a play called *La Disparue – The Missing* (ie deceased) *Woman* – significantly the provisional title for *La Chambre Verte*, where its relevance to the events of the film is clearer than in *Le Dernier Métro*. In the latter film the play-within-the-film is mainly a device enabling Truffaut to air his ideas on love and obsession. Bernard's oft-repeated curtain speech refers back to a similar refrain linked with Catherine Deneuve in her earlier role in *La Sirène du Mississippi*: 'Yes, love hurts. Like a great bird of prey hovering over us, motionless and threatening; but this threat may also be a promise of happiness. You are so beautiful, to look at you is to suffer.'

She: 'Yesterday you said it brought joy.'

He: 'Joy and suffering.'

Still under the impact of these poignant lines we are led into a hospital scene, persuaded that the action has abruptly taken an unexpected turn. Only when we are comprehensively hooked does the camera pull back to reveal that we are witnessing just another play, exactly like the trick opening scene in *La Nuit Américaine*. Inspired by his mentor Renoir, Truffaut has had the confidence to play with our emotions and he has succeeded in getting us to share his delight once more in the artifices of the cinema.

# 24: La Femme d'à Côté

*Le Dernier Métro* was Truffaut's biggest box-office success, winning ten Césars – the French Oscars – to the surprise of the director, who confessed at the award ceremony that he thought he had 'blown the film'. His astonishment and elation at the standing ovation it received paralleled his triumph twenty years earlier with *Les Quatre Cents Coups* at Cannes, the launching pad for his film career. But *Le Dernier Métro*, while never less than charming, is essentially soft-centred and loosely focused, a good old-fashioned star vehicle for the talents of Catherine Deneuve, but not unlike the kind of film he had enjoyed attacking as a young critic in the Fifties.

With *La Femme d'à Côté*, his penultimate film, he tried to do something different. It is not difficult to see what attracted him to the subject of the film, given his fascination with portraying obsessive passions in a whole range of films from *La Mariée était en Noir* to *L'Histoire d'Adèle H.* and *La Chambre Verte*. Nor is it difficult to see why he decided to offer Fanny Ardant, who the year before had been starring in a French TV serial, her first screen role as the 'woman next door' of the title. Truffaut's personal involvement with the actress led to the birth of a child, Joséphine, (his third daughter and her second) and to another starring role for Fanny Ardant in 1983 in his final film *Vivement Dimanche!*. Despite her prolific number of appearances in French films in the mid-Eighties, Fanny Ardant might not be everyone's first choice, unlike say Jeanne Moreau or Catherine Deneuve in their prime, for the crucial femme fatale role in *La Femme d'à Côté*. Truffaut

'torrid passion ... and its tendency to burst forth unpredictably' (Depardieu & Ardant)

for obvious reasons thought otherwise and his camera follows her around devotedly.

The film suffers from a lack of information about the relationship between Bernard (Gérard Depardieu again) and Mathilde (Fanny Ardant) so that it is not clear what they saw in each other several years earlier, why their affair ended nor why their passion continues to smoulder. If, as in classical tragedy, the action occurs at a point when passions have reached a climax and crisis is imminent, then it is possible to dispense with detailed explanations of why A loves B who loves C who loves A and so on. But if this context is dispensed with, then the emotions depicted must be seen to be violent and the passions must be convincingly intense. If on the other hand the whole thing seems to amount to little more than a tennis-club romance, then something has gone wrong.

The success of *La Femme d'à Côté*, as with *L'Argent de Poche*, depends enormously on the extent to which the audience shares, or comes to share, the director's viewpoint. The obsessional factor in

'. . . domestic harmony disrupted' by the 'woman next door'. (Fanny Ardant)

this film is not limited to the behaviour of the actors, it extends beyond them to embrace the way in which the director treats his subject. So intent is Truffaut on focusing on the violent passion being lived out by Bernard and Mathilde, that he seriously neglects to give the necessary credibility to the supporting roles, as happened in *Adèle H*. The relationship between Bernard and his wife Arlette, who live peacefully with their son in a village near Grenole, is never explored. Truffaut depicts only the superficial aspects, the conventional couple's pleasantly bland appearance, while reducing the presence of their son to the purely decorative. The domestic harmony à la *Domicile Conjugal* is disturbed by the sudden appearance in the village of Mathilde, Bernard's old flame. By chance, and here Truffaut stretches the credibility gap, Mathilde and her new old (i.e. recent but mature) husband, Philippe, have just taken the house next door. Jacques Brel's bitter-sweet 'Mathilde est revenue' immediately springs to mind, anticipating his later 'Ne me quitte pas' and references to the volcano that was thought to be extinguished bursting into flame again, truths expressed in songs which are all that Mathilde is able to hold on to by the end.

Having set the scene Truffaut is now free to indulge in a series of gratuitous cinematic allusions. Mathilde is 'The Aviator's Wife – the title of Rohmer's film – though in fact her husband is really an air traffic controller. Those who thought they were in for a Rohmer-style subtle investigation of the nuances of human motivation, passion and guilt are rapidly disillusioned. For we are in Truffaut territory with male heroes seen as always from the female viewpoint. So Bernard is depicted playing with his model boats, like Antoine Doinel and Bertrand Morane in L'Homme qui Aimait les Femmes.

Despite providing no explanation of the previous love affair between Bernard and Mathilde, and no investigation of either of their current marital relationships, Truffaut asks us to accept the uncontrollable nature of their torrid passion and its tendency to burst forth unpredictably. Unfortunately the ensuing action sometimes descends into melodrama and unintentionally into farce. Mathilde faints with alarming regularity at times of emotional crisis. Bernard beats her up in public in a desperate attempt to rekindle her waning passion at one point in their stop–go affair. The melodramatic situation of the two principals is encapsulated within an equally credibility-stretching sub-plot, which involves the narrator, Madame Jouve, whose unrequited love led her to a botched suicide attempt, a subsequent existence as a cripple and a masochistically courageous refusal to burden her former lover, who caused it all, by either telling him the story or accepting his offer of happiness when he returns twenty years later. To cap it all Madame Jouve, à la Piaf, 'has no regrets'.

The film's denouement, after Mathilde's psychiatric treatment during which she learns that 'to be loved one has to be lovable', owes much to La Mariée était en Noir. Both end with shooting, though it does seem a touch gratuitous and insufficiently motivated in La Femme d'à Côté compared with the sense of righteous revenge and the skilfully manipulated intensification of suspense and

'Neither with you nor without you' Bernard (Gérard Depardieu) and Mathilde
(Fanny Ardant)

Truffaut & 'femme fatale' (Fanny Ardant)

feeling of inevitability in *La Mariée*. The official tone and language of the final commentary produces a distancing effect from the intensity of the passions just witnessed: 'In view of the position of the bodies, there is good reason to believe that the man and woman had sexual relationships just before their death.' We recall the allusion in *Les Mistons* to the female praying mantis devouring the male after copulation.

The most frustrating aspect of *La Femme d'à Côté* is its inability to encompass the truly felt tragic dimension within its rather flimsy structure. In some ways the film resembles *Jules et Jim* with Mathilde killing Bernard and then herself, just as Catherine engulfed herself and Jim in death. Mathilde like Bernard is a creature of the flesh and the primary raison d'être of their relationship is sexual. Contrary to his normal practice Truffaut shows the couple in the act of love-making, though it is significant that neither of the two married couples is ever depicted in a similar situation. Mathilde, pregnant by Bernard earlier, had an abortion. The sad truth of her accusation: 'You wanted a child, but not by me and you had one by another woman,' reminds us that Mathilde and Bernard, like Catherine and Jim, have failed to create a child between them and in Truffaut's universe lack of fertility is always a threat to the happiness of a couple. Prisoners of their passion, Mathilde and Bernard are doomed to die. In the film's final coda Madame Jouve says she would have chosen for their epitaph: 'Neither with you nor without you', a terrible indictment on the relationship and applicable to Julien Davenne and Julie, Adèle and Pinson and many other doom-laden Truffaut couples. In life Mathilde and Bernard were unable to live without each other and unable to live with each other. Their bodies are fused in the act of making love and then in death. Just as in *Jules et Jim* Jules had dreamed of mingling the ashes of Catherine and Jim, but it was not allowed, so here for the same reason Madame Jouve fears that the bodies of Mathilde and Bernard will not be placed in the same tomb. There is no guarantee of harmony even in death.

# 25: Vivement Dimanche!

Such harmony as there is within Truffaut's universe is not to be found in death, and only intermittently in life, other than inside the closed world of film-making. As the director, played by Truffaut, in *La Nuit Américaine* says: 'Films ... are more harmonious than life ... Personal problems no longer count. The cinema reigns.' Truffaut's last film *Vivement Dimanche!* communicates his infectious joy in the film-making process and demonstrates his mastery of the medium.

There are few tasks harder for a French director than to produce a convincing French version of an American thriller. The American 'série noire' has its own specific conventions that transfer badly or not at all to the French context. In *Tirez sur le Pianiste* Truffaut accomplished the difficult feat with David Goodis's *Down There* by acknowledging the conventions of the genre while simultaneously subverting them with his idiosyncratic brand of off-beat humour and comic improvisation, to the delight of cinephiles the world over.

*Vivement Dimanche!* ventures into the same territory but solves the problem of the transposition to a French setting in a slightly different way. The film is an adaptation of Charles Williams' *The Long Saturday Night*, which partly explains the title chosen by Truffaut – *Vivement Dimanche!*, which translates as *Finally Sunday!* or more precisely *Roll on Sunday!* – the sense of which, as with the title of *La Sirène du Mississippi*, is rather obscured in the film version of the novel. Truffaut manages to create a cinematic universe from which almost all allusions to an external

Julien (Jean-Louis Trintignant) and Marie-Christine, his unfaithful wife (Caroline Sihol)

Fanny Ardant, filmed by Truffaut with delicacy and delight

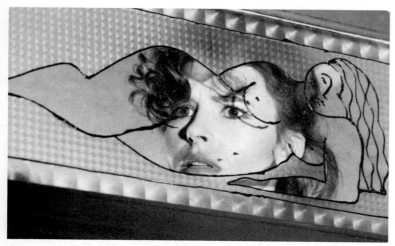

Barbara on the trail in the night-club (Ardant)

geographical reality are rigorously excluded. There is no sense of place: anonymous locations – night-clubs, hotel lobbies, a cinema foyer – could be anywhere. The action is supposed to take place mostly somewhere on the French Riviera but by shooting largely at night – or at least 'day for night' – and in pouring rain, the sense of anonymity is enhanced. So we may be in the world of the American-style thriller but it is a world from which everything specifically American has been eliminated.

The setting in any event is of no importance. Its artificiality at times borders on the abstract. Nor is the unravelling of the plot, the police investigation, of any interest to Truffaut. What does excite him is the creation of a world of marvellous comic invention and artifice out of nothing. His pleasure lies in Hitchcock-style manipulation, pulling the strings of his creations for the sheer pleasure of propelling them into each other's arms. His achievement is to get us to believe in the reality of the criminal investigation while simultaneously getting us to stand outside the crime thriller convention and to share his pleasure as he mocks it with a nudge and a wink. And this is no mean achievement. Another of his famous bets has been won. *Vivement Dimanche!* is smoother and slicker

'Barbara goes off in search of the truth' (Ardant & Trintignant)

than *Tirez sur le Pianiste*, though lacking some of the speed and spontaneity of the earlier film. Perhaps its greater professionalism is simply a reflection of the increased maturity of the director. His ambition may go no higher than to entertain but at least he entertains with style.

For what was to be his final film it is fitting that Truffaut should have returned to his beloved black and white. Apart from being completely in keeping with the thriller genre, the effect is also to add a dimension of mystery and nostalgia and to distance the action in time. It also heightens the beauty of Fanny Ardant, whose role as the secretary in love with her boss, Jean-Louis Trintignant, was written specifically to allow her to demonstrate her talent for comedy after the intensity of *La Femme d'à Côté*. Truffaut always enjoys showing active, dominant women in contrast to the vulnerable, fragile male and Fanny Ardant's role in this film parallels that of Catherine Deneuve in *Le Dernier Métro*. The role of the secretary in *Vivement Dimanche!* is enhanced to allow her, and not her boss, to conduct the investigation, while he, like Lucas in

Barbara is not entirely convinced of her boss' innocence!

*Le Dernier Métro*, lies in hiding in the cellar, consoling himself à la Bertrand Morane, with staring at the legs of the women who walk past his basement window. If, as Truffaut said, quoting Renoir, back in 1958, 'The film director's task consists of getting pretty women to do pretty things,' then never did he apply the precept more faithfully than in *Vivement Dimanche!*

Much could be written about the recurrence of names in Truffaut. Barbara Becker is the secretary of estate agent Julien Vercel. Becker, apart from the gratuitous link with the film-maker, is also the name of the schoolteacher in *La Mariée* and a variation on the name, Julie Baker, is given to the role played by Jacqueline Bisset in *La Nuit Américaine*. Julien is the name of one of the boys in *L'Argent de Poche* and also recalls Julien Davenne in *La Chambre Verte*, whose dead wife was called Julie. In Truffaut's world the impression given is of being 'en famille'. Julien is accused of a number of murders (including that of his unfaithful wife) and Barbara, although not entirely convinced at the outset of her boss' innocence, goes off in search of the truth. Truffaut speaks elsewhere of the way little-known writers of crime fiction often reveal themselves

213

in intimate detail in their writing, secure in the illusion that they remain anonymous behind the corpses and shootings with which their plots are littered. Likewise Truffaut, thinly concealed behind the tortuous plot of *Vivement Dimanche!*, reveals his own tenderness, his relish for the intimate details of human behaviour, his pleasure in setting his characters one against the other and also in bringing them together again, his delicacy and delight in filming the vulnerability and also the beauty of women. No longer does he need to appear in his films in the guise of Jean-Pierre Léaud. He is present throughout *Vivement Dimanche!* and his presence, his sense of freedom, his complicity with the audience and his 'joie de vivre' pervade the film.

*Vivement Dimanche!* contains a succession of homages to the crime thriller in general, the 1940s gangster film, the American comedy and a series of quotations from Renoir, Hitchcock, Resnais and Truffaut himself. Cinephiles have fun but so too do the general public, unaware of most of the allusions, but accepting them as original gags integrated into the fabric of the film. Truffaut's tribute to the masters of the kind of cinema he most loved and consistently praised is sometimes a little slow-paced, despite the bewildering twists of the plot, as if he needed to linger nostalgically over each homage.

*Vivement Dimanche!* is neither innovative nor revolutionary but then Truffaut never laid claim to either of these qualities. All he ever wished to do was to revisit the cinema he loved and to make films in the same vein. His ambition in *Vivement Dimanche!* is modestly restricted to a desire to please and to entertain, but such is the virtuosity of his display of light-hearted verve and joyful panache that the classification of the comedy thriller as a minor genre must after this film be open to question.

# 26: Finally Truffaut

*Finally Sunday!*, the title of *Vivement Dimanche!* in Great Britain – in the USA it is called *Confidentially Yours* – is a grimly appropriate title for Truffaut's last film since it was on a Sunday – 21 October 1984 – that he died.

With a self-appointed total of thirty films to make, he had reached a point only three-quarters of the way through, and had always believed that 'You don't die until your work is finished.' Though Truffaut had known for some weeks that death was near, and his intimates had known for several months that his brain tumour was incurable, the end when it came was neither swift nor dignified.

Finally, on the Sunday, came the news and with it both relief and anger – that he should have died at the age of fifty-two, the same age as his mother, with so many unfinished projects and so much still to accomplish. Antoine's phrase in *L'Amour en Fuite* is totally applicable to Truffaut: 'My life is compartmentalized.' He habitually worked on up to four films simultaneously and was obsessive about scrupulously planning his time and mapping out his life years ahead. He aimed to make on average one film per year, knowing that as he was completing one, there was always another in the pipeline. The maturation process for some of his films, like *Adèle H.* and *La Chambre Verte*, took a number of years. It was almost as if Truffaut believed that by immersing himself in his programme of work he would somehow be immune from death.

Fearing he would no longer have the stamina to continue to

make films much beyond the age of sixty, Truffaut planned to cease directing after his thirtieth film and to devote himself to writing. At the time of his death three or four film projects were in varying stages of development, others existed on file, others had been provisionally or definitively abandoned and others were hardly beyond the initial concept stage. There were also notes for a provisionally abandoned book about actors and some tapes recorded by Claude de Givray during the final months containing Truffaut's account of his early life for possible integration into his autobiography.

In 1977 while acting in Spielberg's *Close Encounters of the Third Kind*, Truffaut began taking notes for a possible book on the life of actors. 'I experienced what actors go through when I ask them to film with me: the waiting, the agony, the time wasted, the fear of performing badly, the obsession with trivia, the pleasure of being told what to do and the boredom ... Actors work "against" the director and vice versa. The director is afraid of his work being ruined; actors think they are more important than the film ... The book will be called *Actors Waiting* ... Actors spend their time waiting ... I very quickly felt wretched at having to bear all this nerve-fraying waiting. It's debasing ... I saw actors pacing up and down as if they were in a prison corridor ... I felt transformed into an actor. I would even say I felt myself become a woman in every sense. I wanted Spielberg to be pleased and I experienced a certain pleasure in getting him to like me ... Acting is a state of frustration mixed with pleasure. The pleasure is in the limited responsibility ... There are no decisions to make ... I will never work for anyone else again. The frustration is too great. One is not in control of events.'

Truffaut had already decided to shelve his book on actors. It joins the ranks of the might-have-beens, along with the projected autobiography, that will now never be written. In the same category are a number of film projects which might have been developed, or in some cases resuscitated, but which now will go no further, unless Suzanne Schiffman, Claude de Givray or Jean Gruault feel able or willing to direct these films.

A very sketchy idea for a film about a lady-killer, à la Monsieur Verdoux, was under discussion with Claude de Givray in the months before Truffaut's death. Guy Marchand was envisaged –

216

though not contacted – for the part of the killer and the action was to take place in the perfume industry in Grasse on the French Riviera. Claude de Givray was to interview perfume manufacturers and Truffaut sent him several books on crime, but the project never developed beyond this embryonic stage.

Other vague projects involving Jean Gruault adapting novels by Kleist and William Irish were never developed nor was a film about a little boy who succeeds to the throne, to be called *Le Petit Roi*. A more developed project with Gruault was called *Julien et Marguerite*, based on a real-life story of incest in the reign of Henry IV and also the *Chroniques Italiennes* of Stendhal. Gruault was working on this in 1972 and a version annotated by Truffaut exists but the project had already been abandoned, though it might have resurfaced later.

A more recent project under serious consideration was an adaptation of La Varende's *Nez-de-Cuir*, for which Truffaut had bought the film rights, in the hope of continuing the successful Depardieu/Ardant pairing from *La Femme d'à Côté*. Depardieu would have played the wealthy, aristocratic landowner, a Don Juan figure adored by women, who goes off to fight in the Napoleonic wars, gets his face horribly mutilated and is left for dead. However he survives, has a leather mask made to cover the hole in his face, and falls in love … with Fanny Ardant, for whom a specially strong role was to be created, combining two of the parts in the novel, as was done on a larger scale for Jeanne Moreau in *Jules et Jim*. Claude de Givray and Truffaut worked on *Nez-de-Cuir* in 1984 in an effort to strengthen the dramatic movement and also to reach a decision about the hunting scenes, which could not be assimilated happily into Truffaut's intimate personal universe. At the time of Truffaut's death thirty pages of the synopsis existed but problems remained.

Of three other projects on the drawing-board, an untitled work on France from 1900 to 1914 was by far the most ambitious and demanding. Inspired by Forman's *Ragtime* and Bergman's *Fanny and Alexander*, Truffaut and Jean Gruault had begun work on it in 1982. But Truffaut soon showed signs of going off the project, partly because of the inherent demands of a big budget, large-scale period production and partly because of the release of other films on a similar theme, such as Lelouch's *Les Uns et Les Autres*. The idea was to make a saga showing the lives of a group of characters, both real and imaginary, between 1900 and the outbreak of World War One. The characters would have children who would themselves be the subject of subsequent films set in the Twenties and Thirties and the cycle would culminate in the Forties with *Le Dernier Métro*. Proust was set to encounter Fanny Ardant while Depardieu was to play a wealthy industrialist, modelled on the automobile pioneer Louis Renault, but in his case responsible for the invention of the escalator, whose Chaplinesque comic potential excited Truffaut and Gruault. The shooting script is characteristically flat with Truffaut as usual only writing down the things he was afraid of forgetting and not bothering to record what was clearly fixed in his mind. Consequently, as on most of his films, only he and Suzanne Schiffman had any detailed idea of where the film was going and even that was always subject to modification. Despite this, the film is perhaps the only one of Truffaut's unfinished projects which it might be possible for somebody else to make, with a lot of help from Jean Gruault and Suzanne Schiffman.

Another project on which work was in progress in 1983 was *L'Agence Magic*, for which Bernard Revon and Claude de Givray had provided a preliminary treatment back in 1976 – one hundred and forty pages of typed manuscript, interspersed with Truffaut's copious, handwritten annotations. This film was also to link with *Le Dernier Métro*, being part of a trilogy on the world of entertainment and doing for the music-hall what *La Nuit Américaine* had done for film-making and *Le Dernier Métro* for the theatre. Truffaut was not completely happy with the project, partly because it involved a complicated and expensive location shoot in Africa and partly because he was more immediately excited by the prospect of filming a well-matured project, *La Petite Voleuse*, which, had he lived, would have become his twenty-second feature.

*L'Agence Magic* (the spelling is deliberately anglicized, though the significance of the title and its relevance to the film, not for the first time with Truffaut, is not absolutely clear, not even to Claude de Givray) is a melodrama about a troupe of music-hall artistes on tour in North Africa. The company, which includes a tight-rope walker, a magician and a specialist in the imitation of automatons, is managed by a mature woman – Jeanne Moreau was envisaged for the part – who is the mistress of an African Minister of Culture.

When the regime collapses, the survival of the troupe is threatened.

One member of the troupe, a girl in her late teens, does an act in which her life is at risk every night. She is also something of a nymphomaniac, until she falls in love with the 'automaton', who promises to marry her but then changes his mind and leaves her. Jealous and in despair, the girl kills him in a fit of 'dépit amoureux'. Her mother, who is the director of the troupe and who has shared everything with her daughter, including some of her earlier men, pleads guilty to the crime and the film ends with her sublime act of self-sacrifice. The Hitchcockian device of depicting characters who have a secret, or an element of mystery in their lives, is linked with Renoir's oft-quoted maxim about people always having their reasons, by two episodes in the film. The first concerns the young girl, whose sexual hyperactivity and need to take risks are 'explained' as compensatory mechanisms, assertions of the life force in the face of infirmity, in this case the polio from which she had suffered as a child. It is also revealed that the 'automaton', whose secret exchange of letters has aroused the girl's jealousy, is in fact following a correspondence course in religious education, having at the age of seven witnessed his mother's suicide and having been struck dumb for two years.

Truffaut later decided to set the film in south-west France during the German Occupation, thereby avoiding the complications and the expense of the African dimension. The script as usual is not over-rich as Truffaut again had all the essential dialogue in his head. Claude de Givray has no doubts that the film would somehow have been made.

There are even fewer doubts about the fact that his next feature would however have been *La Petite Voleuse*, on which Truffaut's file dates back to 1959. The film is the story of Janine, a tomboyish thief, aged fifteen at the beginning of the film and seventeen at the end, who steals cigarettes from American soldiers in France in the early Fifties, progresses to the theft of a music box and ends up in a reformatory. The story comprises Truffaut's customary mixture of press clippings, stories of friends, fictional invention and autobiographical elements, depending in particular on a real-life encounter with a young girl in the early Fifties. The script exists in the form of a forty-page synopsis with the crucial dialogue, as always, in Truffaut's head. The film would have been the female version of *Les Quatre Cents Coups* with Janine running away from home at the beginning and being confined in the Villejuif Centre for Juvenile Delinquents, just like Antoine Doinel and his creator. One sequence in the reformatory showing Janine binding books in a workshop is an exact parallel of Truffaut's experience, no doubt casting light on his subsequent almost fetishistic pleasure in the handling of books and fascination with their tangible aspect, as in *Fahrenheit 451*. Unsurprisingly, for one who regarded the ostentatious display of wealth as a positive incitement to crime, Truffaut makes no judgments on theft. In fact, as in *Les Quatre Cents Coups*, he makes no explicit judgments at all. One striking incident, based on an article he had read in *Détective* in the Sixties, depicts Janine's mother stabbing her husband to death in bed. His death is infinitely drawn out, as, apparently not realizing he is dying, he first staggers to the kitchen to get a glass of water, before finally succumbing, with a look of comic amazement.

In his films, Truffaut deliberately underplays the drama and the solemnity of death. He confronted his own death in similar fashion, mocking the idea of his indispensability or that of any man. But he leaves an enormous gap, one that is as difficult to fill or conceal, as the hole in the face of the man in *Nez-de-Cuir*.

François Truffaut lives, as in *La Chambre Verte*, in the memories of those who knew him and, more permanently perhaps, through his films, whether he is perceived directly in person or more diffusely as an all-pervading presence. With his death an arbitrary finality is imposed on his work, arbitrary but indisputable. For François Truffaut the battle between the provisional and the definitive is finally over, and all is now definitive.

# Filmography

## François Truffaut

Born Paris, 6 February 1932.
Father, architect; mother, secretary.
Disturbed adolescence; several menial jobs; reform school.
1947 founded own ciné-club and met André Bazin.
Army service 1951, discharged 1953.
Thanks to Bazin, in 1953 began writing for *Cahiers du Cinéma*.
Assistant to Rossellini for two years from 1956.
Married Madeleine Morgenstern in 1957.
1958 established own production company – *Les Films du Carrosse*.
1959 Laura Truffaut born.
1961 Ewa Truffaut born.
1968 Co-treasurer of committee for the defence of the Cinémathèque.
1983 Joséphine born (mother, Fanny Ardant).
Died Neuilly-sur-Seine, 21 October 1984.

*Les Films du Carrosse* produced a number of short films and was involved in the
 production of all Truffaut's films (with the exception of *Fahrenheit 451*) and also:
*Paris nous appartient* – Jacques Rivette 1958
*Le Testament d'Orphée* – Jean Cocteau 1959
*Tire au flanc* – Claude de Givray 1962 (supervised by Truffaut)
*Mata-Hari, agent H21* – Jean-Louis Richard 1964 (dialogue by Truffaut)
*Deux ou trois choses que je sais d'elle* – Jean-Luc Godard 1966
*L'Enfance nue* – Maurice Pialat 1968
*Ma nuit chez Maud* – Eric Rohmer 1969
*La faute de l'abbé Mouret* – Georges Franju 1970
*Le cheval de fer* – Pierre-William Glenn 1973
*Les lolos de Lola* – Bernard Dubois 1975
*Ce gamin-là* – Renaud Victor 1975
*Le beau mariage* – Eric Rohmer 1981

As an actor Truffaut appeared briefly in a few of his own films and also in *Le coup du berger* – Jacques Rivette 1957 and *Tire au flanc* – Claude de Givray 1962. His major appearances were in three of his own films: as Doctor Jean Itard in *L'Enfant Sauvage* 1970, as the film director, Ferrand, in *La nuit américaine* 1973 and as Julien Davenne in *La chambre verte* 1978. His other major role was as the French UFO specialist, Claude Lacombe, in *Close Encounters of the Third Kind* – Steven Spielberg 1976.

As a writer Truffaut contributed to over a dozen newspapers and magazines, and to monographs on Rossellini (Seghers, Paris 1961) and Godard (Seghers, Paris 1963). He wrote prefaces to *What is Cinema* by André Bazin (Univ. California Press 1971); *Jean Renoir* by André Bazin (Champ Libre 1971); *Le Testament d'un Cancre* by Bernard Gheur (Albin Michel 1971); *Charlie Chaplin* by André Bazin (Ed. du Cerf 1973); *La Grande Illusion* by Jean Renoir (Balland 1974); *Le Cinéma de la Cruauté* by André Bazin (Flammarion 1975); *Le Cinéma de l'Occupation et de la Résistance* by André Bazin (Collection 10/18 1975); *Hollywood Directors (1914–1940)* by Richard Koszariski (Oxford University Press 1976); *Le Soleil et les Ombres* by Jean-Pierre Aumont (Ed. J'ai Lu 1977); *Le Cinéma et Moi* by Sacha Guitry (Ramsay 1977); *André Bazin* by Dudley Andrew (Oxford Univ. Press 1978); *Orson Welles* by André Bazin (Harper & Row 1978); *The Book of the Cinema* by Don Allen et al (Mitchell Beazley 1979); *Un Homme à la Caméra* by Nestor Almendros (Hatier 1980); *La Toile d'Araignée* by William Irish (Belfond 1980).

Truffaut wrote the following full-length works: The script of *A bout de souffle*, which he assigned to Jean-Luc Godard in 1959; *Le Cinéma selon Hitchcock* (Laffont 1966), published as Hitchcock (Simon & Schuster, New York 1967 and by Secker & Warburg, London 1968); *Les Aventures d'Antoine Doinel* (Mercure de France 1970) – the scripts of *Les 400 Coups*, *L'Amour à vingt ans*, *Baisers Volés* and *Domicile Conjugal*; *La Nuit Américaine* (script) followed by *Journal de tournage de Fahrenheit 451* (Seghers 1974); *Les Films de ma Vie* (Flammarion 1975) – selected film reviews; *L'Argent de Poche* – ciné-roman (Flammarion 1975); *L'Homme qui Aimait les Femmes* – ciné-roman (Flammarion 1977); *Hitchcock-Truffaut* (Secker & Warburg 1968, revised in 1985)

# Films

### Une Visite (1955)

| | |
|---|---|
| Director | François Truffaut |
| Script | François Truffaut |
| Photography | Jacques Rivette |
| Editors | Alain Resnais, François Truffaut |

With: Florence Doniol-Valcroze, Jean-José Richer, Laura Mauri, Francis Cognany.

Shot on 16 mm in Jacques Doniol-Valcroze's apartment in Paris during 1955.

### Les Mistons (1957)

| | |
|---|---|
| Production Company | Les Films du Carrosse |
| Production Manager | Robert Lachenay |
| Director | François Truffaut |
| Assistant Directors | Claude de Givray, Alain Jeannel |
| Script | François Truffaut. Based on a short story in *Virginales* by Maurice Pons |
| Director of Photography | Jean Malige |
| Editor | Cécile Decugis |
| Music | Maurice Le Roux |
| Narrator | Michel François |

Gérard Blain (*Gérard*), Bernadette Lafont (*Bernadette*), and 'les mistons'.

Filmed on location in Nimes, August–September 1957. First shown at the Tours Film Festival (out of competition), November 1957; Paris, 3 March 1961; GB, 19 January 1961; USA, 1959. Running time, 26 min. (later cut by Truffaut to 17 min.).

Distributors: Les Films de la Pléiade (France), Gala (GB).

GB/US title: THE MISCHIEF MAKERS

### Une Histoire d'Eau (1958)

| | |
|---|---|
| Production Company | Les Films de la Pléiade |
| Producer | Pierre Braunberger |
| Production Manager | Roger Fleytoux |
| Directors | François Truffaut, Jean-Luc Godard |
| Script | Jean-Luc Godard |

| | |
|---|---|
| Director of Photography | Michel Latouche |
| Editor | Jean-Luc Godard |
| Sound | Jacques Maumont |
| Narrator | Jean-Luc Godard |

Jean-Claude Brialy (*The Man*), Caroline Dim (*The Girl*).

Filmed on location in and around Paris, early spring 1958 (filmed by Truffaut, completed by Godard). First shown in Paris, 3 March 1961. Running time, 18 min.

Distributors: Unidex (France), Connoisseur (GB).

## Les Quatre Cents Coups (1959)

| | |
|---|---|
| Production Company | Les Films du Carrosse/SEDIF |
| Production Manager | Georges Charlot |
| Director | François Truffaut |
| Assistant Director | Philippe de Broca |
| Script | François Truffaut |
| Adaptation | François Truffaut, Marcel Moussy |
| Dialogue | Marcel Moussy |
| Director of Photography | Henri Decaë (Dyaliscope) |
| Camera Operator | Jean Rabier |
| Editor | Marie-Josèph Yoyotte |
| Art Director | Bernard Evein |
| Music | Jean Constantin |
| Sound | Jean-Claude Marchetti |

Jean-Pierre Léaud (*Antoine Doinel*), Albert Rémy (*M. Doinel*), Claire Maurier (*Mme Doinel*), Patrick Auffay (*René Bigey*), Georges Flamant (*M. Bigey*), Yvonne Claudie (*Mme Bigey*), Robert Beauvais (*School Director*), Pierre Repp (*Bécassine, the English teacher*), Guy Decomble (*Teacher*), Luc Andrieux (*Gym teacher*), Daniel Couturier, François Nocher and Richard Kanayan (*Children*), Claude Mansard (*Judge*), Jacques Monod (*Commissioner*), Marius Laurey (*Police clerk*), Henri Virlogeux (*Nightwatchman*), Christian Brocard (*Man with typewriter*), Jeanne Moreau (*Woman with dog*), Jean-Claude Brialy (*Man in street*), Jacques Demy (*Policeman*), François Truffaut (*Man in funfair*), Bouchon.

Filmed on location in Paris and Honfleur, 10 November 1958–5 January 1959. First shown at the Cannes Film Festival, May 1959; Paris, 3 June 1959; GB, 3 March 1960 (previously at London Film Festival, November 1959); USA, December 1959. Running time, 94 min. (released in 1967 in France in a longer version, running time 101 min.).

Distributors: Cocinor (France), Curzon (GB; currently distributed in a dubbed version by Gala), Zenith (USA).

## Tirez sur le Pianiste (1960)

| | |
|---|---|
| Production Company | Les Films de la Pléiade |
| Producer | Pierre Braunberger |
| Production Manager | Roger Fleytoux |
| Director | François Truffaut |
| Assistant Directors | Francis Cognany, Robert Bober |
| Script | François Truffaut, Marcel Moussy. Based on the novel *Down There* by David Goodis |
| Dialogue | François Truffaut |
| Director of Photography | Raoul Coutard (Dyaliscope) |
| Camera Operator | Claude Beausoleil |
| Editors | Cécile Decugis, Claudine Bouché |
| Art Director | Jacques Mély |
| Music | Georges Delerue |
| Songs: | |
| 'Dialogues d'amoureux' | Félix Leclerc; sung by Félix Leclerc, Lucienne Vernay |
| 'Framboise' | Bobby Lapointe; sung by Bobby Lapointe |
| Sound | Jacques Gallois |

Charles Aznavour (*Edouard Saroyan/Charlie Kohler*), Marie Dubois (*Léna*), Nicole Berger (*Thérésa*), Albert Rémy (*Chico Saroyan*), Claude Mansard (*Momo*), Daniel Boulanger (*Ernest*), Michèle Mercier (*Clarisse*), Richard Kanayan (*Fido Saroyan*), Jean-Jacques Aslanian (*Richard Saroyan*), Serge Davri (*Plyne*), Claude Heymann (*Lars Schmeel*), Alex Joffé (*Stranger*), Catherine Lutz (*Mammy*), Bobby Lapointe (*Singer*).

Filmed in Paris and Le Sappey near Grenoble, 30 November 1959–22 January 1960 (some scenes re-shot during March 1960). First shown in Paris, 25 November 1960; GB, 8 December 1960 (previously at London Film Festival, 21 October 1960); USA, 24 July 1962. Running time, 80 min.

Distributors: Cocinor (France), Gala (GB), Astor (USA).
GB title: SHOOT THE PIANIST; US title: SHOOT THE PIANO PLAYER


## Jules et Jim (1961)

| | |
|---|---|
| Production Company | Les Films du Carrosse/SEDIF |
| Production Manager | Marcel Berbert |
| Director | François Truffaut |
| Assistant Directors | Georges Pellegrin, Robert Bober |
| Script | François Truffaut, Jean Gruault. Based on the novel by Henri-Pierre Roché |
| Director of Photography | Raoul Coutard (Franscope) |
| Camera Operator | Claude Beausoleil |
| Editor | Claudine Bouché |

| | |
|---|---|
| Music | Georges Delerue |
| Song: | |
| 'Le Tourbillon' | Boris Bassiak; sung by Jeanne Moreau |
| Costumes | Fred Capel |
| Narrator | Michel Subor |

Jeanne Moreau (*Catherine*), Oskar Werner (*Jules*), Henri Serre (*Jim*), Marie Dubois (*Thérèse*), Vanna Urbino (*Gilberte*), Sabine Haudepin (*Sabine*), Boris Bassiak (*Albert*), Kate Noëlle (*Birgitta*), Anny Nielsen (*Lucy*), Christiane Wagner (*Helga*), Jean-Louis Richard and Michel Varesano (*Customers in café*), Pierre Fabre (*Drunk in café*), Danielle Bassiak (*Albert's friend*), Bernard Largemains (*Merlin*), Elen Bober (*Mathilde*), Dominique Lacarrière (*Woman*).

Filmed in and around Paris, Alsace and St Paul de Vence, 10 April–3 June 1961. First shown in Paris, 23 January 1962; GB, 17 May 1962; USA, May 1962. Running time, 105 min.

Distributors: Cinédis (France); Gala (GB); Janus Films (USA).
GB/US title: JULES AND JIM

## *Antoine et Colette* (episode in *L'Amour à Vingt Ans*) (1962)

| | |
|---|---|
| Production Company | Ulysse Productions/Unitel |
| Producer | Pierre Roustang |
| Production Manager | Philippe Dussart |
| Director | François Truffaut |
| Artistic Adviser | Jean de Baroncelli |
| Assistant Director | Georges Pellegrin |
| Script | François Truffaut |
| Dialogue | Yvon Samuel |
| Director of Photography | Raoul Coutard (Franscope) |
| Camera Operator | Claude Beausoleil |
| Editor | Claudine Bouché |
| Music | Georges Delerue, Yvon Samuel (lyrics) |
| Lyrics | sung by Xavier Despras |
| Narrator | Henri Serre |

Jean-Pierre Léaud (*Antoine Doinel*), Marie-France Pisier (*Colette*), François Darbon (*Colette's father*), Rosy Varte (*Colette's mother*), Patrick Auffay (*René*), Jean-François Adam (*Albert Tazzi*).

Filmed in Paris, November 1971. First shown in Paris and at Berlin Film Festival, 22 June 1962; GB, 10 September 1964; USA, March 1963.

Distributors: 20th Century-Fox (France/GB); Embassy (USA).
GB/US title: LOVE AT TWENTY

## La Peau Douce (1964)

| | |
|---|---|
| Production Company | Les Films du Carrosse/SEDIF |
| Production Manager | Marcel Berbert |
| Director | François Truffaut |
| Assistant Director | Jean-François Adam |
| Script | François Truffaut, Jean-Louis Richard |
| Dialogue | François Truffaut |
| Director of Photography | Raoul Coutard |
| Camera Operator | Claude Beausoleil |
| Editor | Claudine Bouché |
| Music | Georges Delerue |

Jean Desailly (*Pierre Lachenay*), Françoise Dorléac (*Nicole Chomette*), Nelly Benedetti (*Franca Lachenay*), Daniel Ceccaldi (*Clément*), Laurence Badie (*Ingrid*), Jean Lanier (*Michel*), Paule Emanuele (*Odile*), Sabine Haudepin (*Sabine*), Gérard Poirot (*Franck*), Georges de Givray (*Nicole's Father*), Carnero (*Organiser at Lisbon*), Dominique Lacarrière (*Pierre's secretary*), Philippe Dumat (*Cinema Manager*), Maurice Garrel (*Bookseller*), Pierre Risch (*Canon*), Charles Lavialle (*Night porter at Hotel Michelet*), Mme Harlaut (*Mme Leloix*), Olivia Poli (*Mme Bontemps*), Catherine Duport (*Young girl at Rheims*), Thérèsa Renouard (*Cashier*), Brigitte Zhendre-Laforest (*Linen delivery woman*), Jean-Louis Richard (*Man in street*).

Filmed in Paris, Orly, Rheims and Lisbon, 21 October–31 December 1963. First shown in Paris (and at Cannes Film Festival), 10 May 1964; GB, 5 November 1964; USA, October 1964. Running time, 115 min.

Distributors: Athos Films (France), Gala (GB), Cinema V (USA).
GB title: SILKEN SKIN; US title: THE SOFT SKIN

## Fahrenheit 451 (1966)

| | |
|---|---|
| Production Company | Anglo Enterprise/Vineyard Films |
| Producer | Lewis M. Allen |
| Associate Producer | Michael Delamar |
| Production Manager | Ian Lewis |
| Director | François Truffaut |
| Assistant Director | Bryan Coates |
| Script | François Truffaut. Based on the novel by Ray Bradbury |
| Additional Dialogue | David Rudkin, Helen Scott |
| Director of Photography | Nicolas Roeg |
| Colour Process | Technicolor |
| Camera Operator | Alex Thompson |
| Editor | Thom Noble |
| Design and Costume Consultant | Tony Walton |

| | |
|---|---|
| Art Director | Syd Cain |
| Special Effects | Bowie Films, Rank Films Processing Division, Charles Staffel |
| Music | Bernard Herrmann |
| Associate Costume Designer | Yvonne Blake |
| Sound Editor | Norman Wanstall |
| Sound Recordists | Bob McPhee, Gordon McCallum |

Oskar Werner (*Montag*), Julie Christie (*Linda/Clarisse*), Cyril Cusack (*The Captain*), Anton Diffring (*Fabian*), Bee Duffell (*The Book-woman*), Gillian Lewis (*TV Announcer*), Jeremy Spenser (*The Man with the apple*), Ann Bell (*Doris*), Caroline Hunt (*Helen*), Anna Palk (*Jackie*), Roma Milne (*Neighbour*), Arthur Cox (*1st Male Nurse*), Eric Mason (*2nd Male Nurse*), Noel Davis and Donald Pickering (*TV Announcers*), Michael Mundell (*Stoneman*), Chris Williams (*Black*), Gillian Aldam (*Judoka woman*), Edward Kaye (*Judoka man*), Mark Lester (*1st small boy*), Kevin Elder (*2nd small boy*), Joan Francis (*Bar Telephonist*), Tom Watson (*Sergeant Instructor*), Alex Scott (*The Life of Henry Brulard*), Dennis Gilmore (*Martian Chronicles*), Fred Cox (*Pride*), Frank Cox (*Prejudice*), Michael Balfour (*Machiavelli's The Prince*), Judith Drynan (*Plato's Republic*), David Glover (*The Pickwick Papers*), Yvonne Blake (*The Jewish Question*), John Rae (*The Weir of Hermiston*), Earl Younger (*Nephew of The Weir of Hermiston*).

Filmed at Pinewood Studios, London, and on location near London (Roehampton, Black Park) and at Châteauneuf-sur-Loire, France, 10 January–28 April 1966. First shown in Paris, 16 September 1966 (previously at Venice Film Festival, September 1966); GB, 18 November 1966; USA, November 1966. Running time, 112 min.

Distributors: Rank (GB), Universal (France/USA).


## La Mariée était en Noir (1967)

| | |
|---|---|
| Production Company | Les Films du Carrosse/Artistes Associés (Paris)/Dino De Laurentiis Cinematografica (Rome) |
| Producer | Marcel Berbert |
| Production Manager | Georges Charlot |
| Director | François Truffaut |
| Assistant Director | Jean Chayrou |
| Script | François Truffaut, Jean-Louis Richard. Based on the novel *The Bride Wore Black* by William Irish [Cornell Woolrich] |
| Director of Photography | Raoul Coutard |
| Colour Process | Eastman Colour |
| Camera Operator | Georges Liron |
| Editor | Claudine Bouché |
| Art Director | Pierre Guffroy |

| Music | Bernard Herrmann |
|---|---|
| Musical Director | André Girard |
| Sound | René Levert |

Jeanne Moreau (*Julie Kohler*), Claude Rich (*Bliss*), Jean-Claude Brialy (*Corey*), Michel Bouquet (*Coral*), Michel Lonsdale (*René Morane*), Charles Denner (*Fergus*), Daniel Boulanger (*Delvaux*), Serge Rousseau (*David*), Alexandra Stewart (*Mlle Becker*), Christophe Bruno (*Cookie Morane*), Jacques Robiolles (*Charlie*), Luce Fabiole (*Julie's mother*), Sylvie Delannoy (*Mme Morane*), Jacqueline Raillard (*Maid*), Van Doude (*Inspector Fabri*), Paul Pavel (*Mechanic*), Gilles Quéant (*Examining Magistrate*), Maurice Garrel (*Plaintiff*), Frédérique and Renaud Fontanarosa (*Musicians*), Elisabeth Rey (*Julie as a child*), Jean-Pierre Rey (*David as a child*), Dominique Robier (*Sabine*), Michèle Viborel (*Gilberte, Bliss' fiancée*), Michèle Montfort (*Model*), Daniel Pommereulle (*Fergus' friend*).

Filmed in and around Paris and in Versailles, Chevilly-Larue, Senlis and Cannes, 16 May–24 July 1967. First shown in Paris, 17 April 1968; GB, 1 August 1968; USA, June 1968. Running time, 107 min.

Distributors: United Artists (France/GB), Lopert (USA).

GB/US title: THE BRIDE WORE BLACK

## *Baisers Volés* (1968)

| Production Company | Les Films du Carrosse/Les Productions Artistes Associés |
|---|---|
| Producer | Marcel Berbert |
| Production Manager | Claude Miler |
| Director | François Truffaut |
| Assistant Directors | Jean-José Richer, Alain Deschamps |
| Script | François Truffaut, Claude de Givray, Bernard Revon |
| Director of Photography | Denys Clerval |
| Colour Process | Eastman Colour |
| Camera Operator | Jean Chiabaut |
| Editor | Agnès Guillemot |
| Art Director | Claude Pignot |
| Music | Antoine Duhamel |
| Song: 'Que reste-t-il de nos amours?' | Charles Trenet; sung by Charles Trenet |
| Sound | René Levert |

Jean-Pierre Léaud (*Antoine Doinel*), Delphine Seyrig (*Fabienne Tabard*), Claude Jade (*Christine Darbon*), Michel Lonsdale (*M. Tabard*), Harry Max (*M. Henri*), André Falcon (*M. Vidal*), Daniel Ceccaldi (*M. Darbon*), Claire Duhamel (*Mme Darbon*), Paul Pavel (*M. Julien*), Serge Rousseau (*The Stranger*), Catherine Lutz (*Mme Catherine*), Jacques Delord (*Conjuror*), Simono (*M. Albani*), Roger Trapp (*Hotel Manager*), Jacques Rispal (*M. Colin*), Martine Brochard (*Mme Colin*),

229

(*Hotel Manager*), Jacques Rispal (*M. Colin*), Martine Brochard (*Mme Colin*), Robert Cambourakis (*Mme Colin's lover*), Marie-France Pisier (*Colette Tazzi*), Jean-François Adam (*Albert Tazzi*), Christine Pellé (*Secretary at Blady agency*), Jacques Robiolles (*Writer*), François Darbon (*Adjutant*), Marcel Mercier and Joseph Merieau (*Men at garage*).

Filmed in and around Paris, 5 February–28 March 1968. First shown at the Avignon Film Festival, 14 August 1968; Paris, 6 September 1968; GB, 27 March 1969 (previously at London Film Festival, 4 December 1968); USA, February 1969. Running time, 91 min.

Distributors: United Artists (France/GB), Lopert Pictures (USA).
GB/US title: STOLEN KISSES

## La Sirène du Mississippi (1969)

| | |
|---|---|
| Production Company | Les Films du Carrosse/Les Productions Artistes Associés (Paris)/Produzioni Associate Delphos (Rome) |
| Producer | Marcel Berbert |
| Production Manager | Claude Miler |
| Director | François Truffaut |
| Assistant Director | Jean-José Richer |
| Script | François Truffaut. Based on the novel *Waltz into Darkness* by William Irish [Cornell Woolrich] |
| Director of Photography | Denys Clerval (Dyaliscope) |
| Colour Process | Eastman Colour |
| Camera Operator | Jean Chiabaut |
| Editor | Agnès Guillemot |
| Art Director | Claude Pignot |
| Music | Antoine Duhamel |
| Sound | René Levert |

Jean-Paul Belmondo (*Louis Mahé*), Catherine Deneuve (*Julie Roussel/Marion*), Michel Bouquet (*Comolli*), Nelly Borgeaud (*Berthe Roussel*), Marcel Berbert (*Jardine*), Roland Thénot (*Richard*), Martine Ferrière (*Landlady*), Yves Drouhet.

Filmed in Réunion, Antibes, Aix-en-Provence, Lyon and near Grenoble, 2 December 1968–February 1969. First shown in Paris, 18 June 1969; GB, Edinburgh Film Festival, 6 September 1970; USA, April 1970. Running time, 123 min.

Distributors: United Artists (France/GB/USA).
US title: MISSISSIPPI MERMAID

## L'Enfant Sauvage (1969)

| | |
|---|---|
| Production Company | Les Films du Carrosse/Les Productions Artistes Associés |
| Producer | Marcel Berbert |

| | |
|---|---|
| Associate Producer | Christian Lentretien |
| Production Manager | Claude Miler |
| Director | François Truffaut |
| Assistant Director | Suzanne Schiffman |
| Script | François Truffaut, Jean Gruault. Based on *Mémoire et Rapport sur Victor de l'Aveyron* by Jean Itard (1806) |
| Director of Photography | Nestor Almendros |
| Camera Operator | Philippe Théaudière |
| Editor | Agnès Guillemot |
| Art Director | Jean Mandaroux |
| Music | Antonio Vivaldi; played by Michel Sanvoisin (recorder) and André Saint-Clivier (mandolin) |
| Musical Adviser | Antoine Duhamel |
| Costumes | Gitt Magrini |
| Sound | René Levert |

Jean-Pierre Cargol (*Victor de l'Aveyron*), François Truffaut (*Dr Jean Itard*), Françoise Seignier (*Mme Guérin*), Jean Dasté (*Professor Philippe Pinel*), Pierre Fabre (*Orderly at Institute*), Paul Villé (*Rémy*), Claude Miler (*M. Lémeri*), Annie Miler (*Mme Lémeri*), René Levert (*Gendarme*), Jean Mandaroux (*Doctor attending Itard*), Nathan Miler (*Lémeri baby*), Mathieu Schiffman (*Mathieu*), Jean Gruault (*Visitor at Institute*), Robert Cambourakis, Gitt Magrini and Jean-François Stévenin (*Peasants*), Laura Truffaut, Ewa Truffaut, Mathieu Schiffman, Guillaume Schiffman, Frédérique Dolbert, Eric Dolbert, Tounet Cargol, Dominique Levert and Mlle Théaudière (*Children at farm*).

Filmed at Aubiat in the Auvergne and in Paris, 7 July–1 September 1969. First shown in Paris, 25 February 1970; GB, 17 December 1970 (previously at London Film Festival, 18 November 1970); USA, New York Film Festival, 10 September 1970. Running time, 84 min.

Distributors: United Artists (France/GB/USA).
GB/US title: THE WILD CHILD

## *Domicile Conjugal* (1970)

| | |
|---|---|
| Production Company | Les Films du Carrosse/Valoria Films (Paris)/Fida Cinematografica (Rome) |
| Producer | Marcel Berbert |
| Production Manager | Claude Miler |
| Director | François Truffaut |
| Assistant Director | Suzanne Schiffman |
| Script | François Truffaut, Claude de Givray, Bernard Revon |
| Director of Photography | Nestor Almendros |
| Colour Process | Eastman Colour |
| Camera Operator | Emmanuel Machuel |
| Editor | Agnès Guillemot |
| Art Director | Jean Mandaroux |

| Music | Antoine Duhamel |
| Costumes | Françoise Tournafond |
| Sound | René Levert |

Jean-Pierre Léaud (*Claude Roc*) Kika Markham (*Anne Brown*), Stacey Tendeter Berghauer (*Kyoko*), Daniel Ceccaldi (*Lucien Darbon*), Claire Duhamel (*Mme Darbon*), Barbara Laage (*Monique*), Jacques Jouanneau (*Césarin*), Daniel Boulanger (*Tenor*), Sylvana Blasi (*Tenor's Wife*), Claude Véga (*The Strangler*), Pierre Fabre (*Office Romeo*), Billy Kearns (*M. Max, the boss*), Danièle Gérard (*Waitress*), Jacques Robiolles (*Sponger*), Yvon Lec (*Traffic Warden*), Pierre Maguelon (*Bistrot Customer*), Marie Irakane (*Concierge*), Ernest Menzer (*Little man*), Jacques Rispal (*Old solitary*), Guy Pierrault (*SOS employee*), Marcel Mercier and Joseph Merieau (*People in courtyard*), Christian de Tilière (*Senator*), Nicole Félix, Jérôme Richard and Marcel Berbert (*Employees in American company*), Marianne Piketti (*Violin pupil*), Annick Asty (*Violin pupil's mother*), Ada Lonati (*Mme Claude*), Nobuko Mati (*Kyoko's friend*), Iska Khan (*Kyoko's father*), Ryu Nakamura (*Japanese secretary*), Jacques Cottin (*M. Hulot*), Marie Dedieu (*Marie*).

Filmed in and around Paris, 22 January–18 March 1970. First shown in Paris, 1 September 1970; GB, 8 July 1971; USA, January 1971. Running time, 97 min.

Distributors: Valoria Films (France), Columbia (GB/USA).
GB/US title: BED AND BOARD

## Les Deux Anglaises et le Continent (1971)

| Production Company | Les Films du Carrosse/Cinetel |
| Producer | Marcel Berbert |
| Production Manager | Claude Miler |
| Director | François Truffaut |
| Assistant Director | Suzanne Schiffman |
| Script | François Truffaut, Jean Gruault. Based on the novel by Henri-Pierre Roché |
| Director of Photography | Nestor Almendros |
| Colour Process | Eastman Colour |
| Camera Operator | Jean-Claude Rivière |
| Editor | Yann Dedet |
| Art Director | Michel de Broin |
| Music | Georges Delerue |
| Costumes | Gitt Magrini |
| Sound | René Levert |
| Narrator | François Truffaut |

Jean-Pierre Léaud (*Claude Roc*) Kika Markham (*Anne Brown*), Stacey Tendeter (*Muriel Brown*), Sylvia Marriott (*Mrs Brown*), Marie Mansart (*Mme Roc*), Philippe Léotard (*Diurka*), Irène Tunc (*Ruta*), Mark Peterson (*Mr Flint*), David Markham

(*Palmist*), Georges Delerue (*Claude's Business Agent*), Marcel Berbert (*Art dealer*), Annie Miler (*Monique de Montferrand*), Christine Pellé (*Claude's Secretary*), Jeanne Lobre (*Jeanne*), Marie Irakane (*Maid*), Jean-Claude Dolbert (*English policeman*), Anne Levaslot (*Muriel as a child*), Sophie Jeanne (*Clarisse*), René Gaillard (*Taxi driver*), Sophie Baker (*Friend in café*), Laura Truffaut, Ewa Truffaut, Mathieu Schiffman and Guillaume Schiffman (*Children*).

Filmed in Normandy, Vivarais, Jura and around Paris, 28 April–13 July 1971. First shown in Paris, 26 November 1971; GB, 3 August 1972; USA, New York Film Festival, 11 October 1972. Running time, 108 min. (cut by French distributor from 132 min.).

Distributors: Valoria Films (France), Gala (GB).
GB title: ANNE AND MURIEL

## Une Belle Fille Comme Moi (1972)

| | |
|---|---|
| Production Company | Les Films du Carrosse/Columbia |
| Executive Producer | Marcel Berbert |
| Production Manager | Claude Miler |
| Director | François Truffaut |
| Assistant Director | Suzanne Schiffman |
| Script | Jean-Loup Dabadie, François Truffaut. Based on the novel *Such a Gorgeous Kid Like Me* by Henry Farrell |
| Director of Photography | Pierre William Glenn |
| Colour Process | Eastman Colour |
| Camera Operator | Walter Bal |
| Editor | Yann Dedet |
| Art Director | Jean-Pierre Kohut |
| Music | Georges Delerue |
| Costumes | Monique Dury |
| Sound | René Levert |

Bernadette Lafont (*Camille Bliss*), Claude Brasseur (*M. Murène*), Charles Denner (*Arthur*), Guy Marchand (*Sam Golden*), André Dussollier (*Stanislas Previne*), Philippe Léotard (*Clovis Bliss*), Anne Kreis (*Hélène*), Gilberte Geniat (*Isobel Bliss*), Danièle Girard (*Florence Golden*), Martine Ferrière (*Prison Secretary*), Michel Delahaye (*M. Marchal*), Annick Fourgerie (*Schoolmistress*), Gaston Ouvrard (*Old Prison Warder*), Jacob Weizbluth (*Alphonse*).

Filmed in Béziers, Languedoc-Roussillon, 14 February–14 April 1972. First shown in Paris, 13 September 1972; GB, 26 June 1973; USA, March 1973. Running time, 100 mins.

Distributors: Columbia (France/USA), Gala (GB).
GB title: A GORGEOUS BIRD LIKE ME; US title: SUCH A GORGEOUS KID LIKE ME

233

## La Nuit Américaine (1973)

| | |
|---|---|
| Production Company | Les Films du Carrosse/PECF (Paris)/Produzione Internazionale Cinematografica (Rome) |
| Producer | Marcel Berbert |
| Production Manager | Claude Miler |
| Director | François Truffaut |
| Assistant Director | Suzanne Schiffman |
| Script | François Truffaut, Jean-Louis Richard, Suzanne Schiffman |
| Director of Photography | Pierre William Glenn |
| Colour Process | Eastman Colour |
| Editor | Yann Dedet |
| Art Director | Damien Lanfranchi |
| Costumes | Monique Dury |
| Sound | René Levert |

Jacqueline Bisset (*Julie/Pamela*), Valentine Cortese (*Séverine*), Alexandra Stewart (*Stacey*), Jean-Pierre Aumont (*Alexandre*), Jean-Pierre Léaud (*Alphonse*), François Truffaut (*Ferrand*), Jean Champion (*Bertrand*), Nathalie Baye (*Joëlle*), Dani (*Assistant continuity girl*), Bernard Menez (*Property Man*), Nike Arrighi (*Odile*), Gaston Joly (*Gaston*), Jean Panisse (*Arthur*), Maurice Séveno (*TV reporter*), David Markham (*Dr Nelson*), Zénaïde Rossi (*Gaston's wife*), Christophe Vesque (*Boy*), Henry Graham and Marcel Berbert (*Insurers*).

Filmed at the Studio Victorine and on location in Nice, 25 September–December 1972. First shown in Paris, 24 May 1973; USA, New York Film Festival, 28 September 1973. Running time, 120 min.

Distributors: Columbia-Warner (France/GB), Warner Bros. (USA).
GB title: DAY FOR NIGHT

## L'Histoire d'Adèle H. (1975)

| | |
|---|---|
| Production Company | Les Films du Carrosse/Artistes Associés |
| Producer | François Truffaut |
| Production Managers | Marcel Berbert, Claude Miller |
| Director | François Truffaut |
| Assistant Director | Suzanne Schiffman |
| Script | François Truffaut and Jean Gruault, based on the Diary of Adèle Hugo by Frances Vernor Guille |
| Director of Photography | Nestor Almendros |
| Colour Process | Eastman Colour |
| Editor | Yann Dedet |
| Music | Maurice Jaubert (1900–1940) |
| Musical Adviser | François Porcile |
| Costumes | Jacqueline Guyot |

Sound     Jean-Pierre Ruh
Art Director    Jean-Pierre Kohut-Svelko

Isabelle Adjani (*Adèle Hugo*), Bruce Robinson (*Lt. Pinson*), Sylvia Marriott (*Mrs Saunders*), Joseph Blatchley (*Bookseller*), Ivry Gitlis (*hypnotist*), Carl Hathwell (*Pinson's orderly*), Raymond Falla (*Judge Johnstone*), Roger Martin (*Dr Murdock*), Jean-Pierre Leursse (*copyist*), Louise Bourdet (*Victor Hugo's servant*), Cecil de Saus-marez (*M. Lenoir*), Reuben Dorey (*Mr Saunders*), Mme Louise (*Mme Baa*), Mr White (*Colonel*), Ralph Williams (*Canadian*), Clive Gillingham (*Bank Clerk*), Edward Jackson (*O'Brien*), Aurelia Mansion (*Widow with dogs*), Jacques Fréjabue (*Cabinetmaker*), Chantal Durpoix (*Prostitute*), François Truffaut (*Officer*), Thi Loan N'Guyen (*Chinese*), David Foote (*Young Boy*), Geoffrey Crook (*George*).

Filmed in Guernsey and Gorée (Senegal), 8 January–21 March 1975. First shown in Paris, 8 October 1975; GB, 1 September 1977. Running time, 95 mins.

Distributors: Artistes Associés (France), Southbrook International Films Ltd (GB).
GB/US title: THE STORY OF ADELE H.

## L'Argent de Poche (1976)

| | |
|---|---|
| Production Company | Les Films du Carrosse/Artistes Associés |
| Producer | François Truffaut |
| Production Managers | Marcel Berbert, Roland Thénot |
| Director | François Truffaut |
| Assistant Directors | Suzanne Schiffman, Alain Maline |
| Script & Dialogue | François Truffaut, Suzanne Schiffman |
| Director of Photography | Pierre-William Glenn |
| Music | Maurice Jaubert (1900–1940) |
| Song: 'Les enfants s'en-nuient le dimanche' | Chales Trenet |
| Musical Director | Patrice Mestral |
| Colour Process | Eastman Colour |
| Editor | Yann Dedet |
| Art Director | Jean-Pierre Kohut-Svelko |
| Sound | Michel Laurent |

Geory Desmouceaux (*Patrick Desmouceaux*), Philippe Goldman (*Julien Leclou*), Claudio Deluca (*Mathieu Deluca*), Franck Deluca (*Himself*), Richard Golfier (*Him-self*), Laurent Devlaeminck (*Laurent Riffle*), Bruno Staab (*Bruno Rouillard*), Sébastien Marc (*Oscar Doinel*), Sylvie Grézel (*Sylvie*), Pascale Bruchon (*Martine*), Corinne Boucart (*Corinne*), Ewa Truffaut (*Patricia*), Laura Truffaut (*Madeleine Doinel*), Jean-François Stévenin (*Jean-François Richet*), Virginie Thévenet (*Lydie Richet*), Chantal Mercier (*Chantal Petit*), Nicole Félix (*Grégory's mother*), Tania Torrens (*Nadine Riffle*), Francis Devlaeminck (*M. Riffle*), Marcel Berbert (*Head-teacher*), Vincent Touly (*Caretaker*), Christine Pellé (*Mme Leclou*), René Barnerias (*M. Desmouceaux*), Christian Lentretien (*M. Golfier*), Paul Heyraud (*M. Deluca*), Little Grégory (*Himself*), Jean-Marie Carayon (*Sylvie's father*), Kathy Carayon

(*Sylvie's mother*), Jeanne Lobre (*Julien's grandmother*), Yvon Boutina (*Oscar as an adult*), Annie Chevaldonné (*Nurse*), Michel Dissart (*M. Lomay*), Monique Dury (*Florist*), Hélène Jeanbrau (*Doctor*), Roland Thénot (*Librarian*), Thi Loan N'Guyen (*His Wife*), François Truffaut (*Martine's father*), Mathieu and Guillaume Schiffman and the people of the village of Thiers.

Filmed in and around Thiers, Clermont-Ferrand and Vichy, 17 July–9 September 1975. First shown in Paris, 17 March 1976; GB, Jume 1977. Running time, 105 mins.

Distributors: Artistes Associés (France), Gala (GB).

GB/US title: SMALL CHANGE

## L'Homme qui Aimait les Femmes (1977)

| | |
|---|---|
| Production Company | Les Films du Carrosse/Artistes Associés |
| Producer | François Truffaut |
| Production Manager | Marcel Berbert |
| Director | François Truffaut |
| Assistant Directors | Suzanne Schiffman, Alain Maline |
| Script & Dialogue | François Truffaut, Michel Fermaud, Suzanne Schiffman |
| Director of Photography | Nestor Almendros |
| Colour Process | Eastman Colour |
| Music | Maurice Jaubert (1900–1940) |
| Musical Director | Patrice Mestral |
| Editor | Martine Barraqué |
| Art Director | Jean-Pierre Kohut-Svelko |
| Sound | Michel Laurent |

Charles Denner (*Bertrand Morane*), Leslie Caron (*Véra*), Brigitte Fossey (*Geneviève Bigey*), Nelly Borgeaud (*Delphine Grezel*), Geneviève Fontanel (*Hélène*), Nathalie Baye (*Martine Desdoits*), Sabine Glaser (*Bernadette*), Valérie Bonnier (*Fabienne*), Anna Perriter (*Uta, babysitter*), Nella Barbier (*Liliane*), Frédérique Jamet (*Juliette*), Monique Dury (*Mme Duteil*), Martine Chassaing (*Denise*), Roselyne Puyo (*Nicole*), Jean Dasté (*Dr Bicard*), Roger Leenhardt (*M. Bétany*), Henri Agel and Henry-Jean Servant (*Readers*), Rico Lopez (*Customer in restaurant*), Marie-Jeanne Montfajon (*Christine Morane, Bertrand's mother*), Michel Marti (*Bertrand as an Adolescent*), Marcel Berbert (*Dr Grezel*), François Truffaut (*Man at funeral*).

Filmed in and around Montpellier, 19 October 1976–5 January 1977. First shown in Paris, 27 April 1977; GB, 2 November 1978. Running time, 119 mins.

Distributors: Artistes Associés (France), Gala (GB), Almi Pictures (USA)
GB/US title: THE MAN WHO LOVED WOMEN

## La Chambre Verte (1978)

| | |
|---|---|
| Production Company | Les Films du Carrosse/Artistes Associés |
| Producer | François Truffaut |

| | |
|---|---|
| Production Managers | Marcel Berbert, Roland Thénot |
| Director | François Truffaut |
| Assistant Directors | Suzanne Schiffman, Emmanuel Clot |
| Script | François Truffaut, Jean Gruault, based on *The Altar of the Dead, Friends of Friends* and *The Beast in the Jungle* by Henry James |
| Dialogue | Jean Gruault |
| Director of Photography | Nestor Almendros |
| Colour Process | Eastman Colour |
| Music | Maurice Jaubert (1900–1940) |
| Musical Director | Patrice Mestral |
| Art Director | Jean-Pierre Kohut-Svelko |
| Editor | Martine Barraqué |
| Sound | Michel Laurent |

Nathalie Baye (*Cécilia Mandel*), François Truffaut (*Julien Davenne*), Jean Dasté (*Bernard Humbert*), Jean-Pierre Ducos (*Priest*), Monique Dury (*Monique, secretary at 'The Globe'*), Jane Lobre (*Mme Rambaud*), Jean-Pierre Moulin (*Gérard Mazet*), Antoine Vitez (*Bishop's Secretary*), Patrick Maléon (*Georges*), Laurence Ragon (*'Julie Davenne'*), Marcel Berbert (*Dr Jardine*), Christian Lentretien (*Speaker at cemetery*), Annie Miller (*Geneviève, the first Mme Mazet*), Marie Jaoul (*Yvonne, the second Mme Mazet*), Guy d'Ablon (*Wax Dummy Maker*), Anna Paniez (*Little Girl at Piano*), Alphonse Simon (*One-legged Man*), Henri Bienvenu (*Auctioneer*), Thi Loan N'Guyen (*Apprentice Artisan*), Serge Rousseau (*Paul Massigny*), Jean-Claude Gasche (*Policeman*), Martine Barraqué (*Nurse*), Josiane Couëdel (*Nurse at Cemetery*), Jean-Pierre Kohut-Svelko (*Cripple at Auction Room*), Roland Thénot (*Cripple at Cemetery*).

Filmed in Honfleur and Caen (chapel is at Fiquefleur-Equainville), 11 October–27 November 1977. First shown in Paris, 5 April 1978; GB, 10 July 1980. Running time, 94 mins.

Distributors: Artistes Associés (France), Gala (GB), New Horizons Picture Corp. (USA).
GB/US title: THE GREEN ROOM

## *L'Amour en Fuite* (1979)

| | |
|---|---|
| Production Company | Les Films du Carrosse |
| Producer | François Truffaut |
| Production Managers | Marcel Berbert, Roland Thénot |
| Director | François Truffaut |
| Assistant Directors | Suzanne Schiffman, Emmanuel Clot |
| Script & Dialogue | François Truffaut, Marie-France Pisier, Jean Aurel, Suzanne Schiffman |
| Director of Photography | Nestor Almendros |
| Colour Process | Eastman Colour and black and white |
| Art Director | Jean-Pierre Kohut-Svelko |

237

| | |
|---|---|
| Editor | Martine Barraqué |
| Music | Georges Delerue |
| Song | *L'Amour en Fuite*, music by Laurent Voulzy, written and sung by Alain Souchon |
| Sound | Michel Laurent |

Jean-Pierre Léaud (*Antoine Doinel*), Marie-France Pisier (*Colette, ex Tazzi*), Claude Jade (*Christine Doinel*), Dani (*Liliane*), Dorothée (*Sabine Barnerias*), Daniel Mesguich (*Xavier Barnerias*), Julien Bertheau (*M. Lucien*), Rosy Varte (*Colette's Mother*), Marie Henriau (*Divorce Judge*), Jean-Pierre Ducos (*Christine's Lawyer*), Pierre Dios (*M. Renard*), Alain Ollivier (*Judge in Aix*), Monique Dury (*Mme Ida*), Emmanuel Clot (*Friend at Printing Press*), Christian Lentretien (*Pick-up on Train*), Roland Thénot (*Telephone operator*), Julien Dubois (*Alphonse Doinel*), Alexandre Janssen (*Child in Dining-Car*), Chantal Zugg (*Child*).
Filmed in Paris, 29 May–7 July 1978. First shown in Paris, 24 January 1979; GB, June 1980. Running time, 94 mins.

Distributors: AMLF (France), Gala (GB).
GB/US title: LOVE ON THE RUN

## Le Dernier Métro (1980)

| | |
|---|---|
| Production Company | Les Films du Carrosse/Andrea Films/SEDIF/ SFP/TF 1 |
| Producer | François Truffaut |
| Production Manager | Jean-José Richer |
| Director | François Truffaut |
| Assistant Directors | Suzanne Schiffman, Emmanuel Clot, Alain Tasma |
| Script | François Truffaut, Suzanne Schiffman |
| Dialogue | François Truffaut, Suzanne Schiffman, Jean-Claude Grumberg |
| Director of Photography | Nestor Almendros |
| Colour Process | Fujicolor |
| Music | Georges Delerue |
| Editor | Martine Barraqué |
| Art Director | Jean-Pierre Kohut-Svelko |
| Sound | Michael Laurent |

Catherine Deneuve (*Marion Steiner*), Gérard Depardieu (*Bernard Granger*), Jean Poiret (*Jean-Loup Cottins*), Heinz Bennent (*Lucas Steiner*), Andrea Ferréol (*Arlette Guillaume*), Paulette Dubost (*Germaine Fabre*), Sabine Haudepin (*Nadine Marsac*), Jean-Louis Richard (*Daxiat*), Maurice Risch (*Raymond Boursier*), Marcel Berbert (*Merlin*), Richard Bohringer (*Gestapo Officer*), Jean-Pierre Klein (*Christian Léglise*), Franck Pasquier (*Jacquot/Eric*), Rose Thierry (*Jacquot's Mother*), Martine Simonet (*Martine Sénéchal*), Renata (*Greta Borg, Cabaret Singer*), Hénia Ziv (*Yvonne*), Jean-José Richer (*René Bernardini*), Jessica Zucman (*Rosette*), René Dupré (*M. Valentin*), Alain Tasma (*Marc*), Pierre Belot (*Hotel Porter*), Christian Baltauss (*Bernard's Replacement*), Jacob Weizbluth (*Rosen*), Laszlo Szabo (*Lt Bergen*).

238

Filmed in and around Paris, 29 January–18 April 1980. First shown in Paris, 17 September 1980; GB, 16 June 1981. Running time, 128 mins (videocassette, 134 mins).

Distributors: Gaumont (France), Gala (GB), MGM/United Artists (USA).
GB/US title: THE LAST METRO

## La Femme d'à Côté (1981)

| | |
|---|---|
| Production Company | Les Films du Carrosse/TF 1 |
| Producer | François Truffaut |
| Production Manager | Armand Barbault |
| Director | François Truffaut |
| Assistant Directors | Suzanne Schiffman, Alain Tasma |
| Script & Dialogue | François Truffaut, Suzanne Schiffman, Jean Aurel |
| Director of Photography | William Lubtchansky |
| Colour Process | Fujicolor |
| Music | Georges Delerue |
| Editor | Martine Barraqué |
| Art Director | Jean-Pierre Kohut-Svelko |
| Sound | Michel Laurent |

Gérard Depardieu (*Bernard Coudray*), Fanny Ardant (*Mathilde Bauchard*), Henri Garcin (*Philippe Bauchard*), Michèle Baumgartner (*Arlette Coudray*), Roger Van Hool (*Roland Duguet*), Véronique Silver (*Mme Odile Jouve*), Philippe Morier-Genoud (*Doctor*), Olivier Becquaert (*Thomas Coudray*).

Filmed in and around Grenoble, 1 April–15 May 1981 First shown in Paris, 30 September 1981; GB, 17 January 1982. Running time, 106 mins.

Distributors: Gaumont (France), Gala (GB), MGM/United Artists (USA).
GB/US title: THE WOMAN NEXT DOOR

## Vivement Dimanche! (1983)

| | |
|---|---|
| Production Company | Les Films du Carrosse/Films A2/Soprofilms |
| Producer | François Truffaut |
| Production Managers | Armand Barbault, Roland Thénot |
| Director | François Truffaut |
| Assistant Directors | Suzanne Schiffman, Rosine Robiolle, Pascal Deux |
| Script & Dialogue | François Truffaut, Suzanne Schiffman, Jean Aurel. Based on the novel *The Long Saturday Night* (French version – *Vivement Dimanche!*) by Charles Williams |
| Director of Photography | Nestor Almendros |

| Colour Process | Black and white |
|---|---|
| Music | Georges Delerue |
| Editor | Martine Barraqué |
| Art Director | Hilton McConnico |
| Sound | Pierre Gamet |

Fanny Ardant (*Barbara Becker*), Jean-Louis Trintignant (*Julien Vercel*), Jean-Pierre Kalfon (*Jacques Massoulier*), Philippe Laudenbach (*M. Clément*), Philippe Morier-Genoud (*Superintendent Santelli*), Xavier Saint-Macary (*Bertrand Fabre*), Jean-Louis Richard (*Louison*), Caroline Sihol (*Marie-Christine Vercel*), Anik Belaubre (*Cashier at the Eden*), Castel Casti (*Taxidriver*), Yan Dedet (*Angel Face*), Nicole Félix (*Scarred Woman*), Georges Koulouris (*Detective Lablache*), Pascale Pellegrin (*Secretary*), Roland Thénot (*Jambrau*), Pierre Gare (*Inspector Poivert*), Jean-Pierre Kohut-Svelko (*The Slav*).

Filmed in and around Hyères, 4 November–22 December 1982. First shown in Paris, 10 August 1983; GB, London Film Festival, 18 October 1983. Running time, 111 mins.

Distributors: AAA (France), Artificial Eye (GB), Spectrafilm (USA).
GB title: FINALLY SUNDAY! US title: CONFIDENTIALLY YOURS

# Acknowledgments

This book is for Françoise, who helped to make it happen.

I am grateful to everyone at Les Films du Carrosse, especially Madeleine Morgenstern, for giving me unrestricted access to articles, scripts and stills. I should like to thank Suzanne Schiffman, Claude de Givray and Jean Gruault, Truffaut's co-scriptwriters, collaborators and friends, for their generous interviews and insights.

My thanks also to Laura Morris for asking me to write the book and for all her support and encouragement, and to Leslie and Lorraine Gerry for designing the cover.

Stills by courtesy of Les Films du Carrosse, Columbia–Warner, Gala, Rank, 20th Century-Fox, United Artists and the Stills Library of the National Film Archive, London.

240